The Disappearance of Amelia Earhart

New and future titles in the series include:

Alien Abductions

Angels

Atlantis

The Bermuda Triangle

The Devil

The Disappearance of Amelia Earhart

Dragons

Dreams

ESP

The Extinction of the Dinosaurs

Extraterrestrial Life

Fairies

Fortune-Telling

Ghosts

Haunted Houses

Jack the Ripper

The Kennedy Assassination

King Arthur

Life After Death

The Loch Ness Monster

Mysterious Places

Poltergeists

Possessions and Exorcisms

Pyramids

Shamans

Stonehenge

UFOs

Witches

The Mystery Library

The Disappearance of Amelia Earhart

Patricia D. Netzley

LUCENT BOOKS

An imprint of Thomson Gale, a part of The Thomson Corporation

Detroit • New York • San Francisco • San Diego • New Haven, Conn. • Waterville, Maine • London • Munich

With thanks to Raymond Netzley for providing valuable information on navigation and to Matthew, Sarah, and Jacob Netzley for their research assistance and patience.

For more information, contact
Lucent Books
27500 Drake Rd.
Farmington Hills, MI 48331-3535
Or you can visit our Internet site at http://www.gale.com

LIBRARY OF CONGRESS CATALOGING-IN-PUBLICATION DATA

Netzley, Patricia D.
   The Disappearance of Amelia Earhart / by Patricia D. Netzley.
     p. cm. — (The mystery library)
   Includes bibliographical references and index.
   ISBN-1-59018-629-X (hardcover : alk. paper)
   1. Earhart, Amelia, 1897–1937—Juvenile literature. 2. Earhart, Amelia, 1897–1937—Death and burial—Juvenile literature. 3. Women air pilots—United States—Juvenile literature. I. Title. II. Series: Mystery library (Lucent Books)

TL540.E3N47 2004
629.13'092—dc22
                                                     2004019009

Printed in the United States of America

Contents

Foreword

In Shakespeare's immortal play *Hamlet*, the young Danish aristocrat Horatio has clearly been astonished and disconcerted by his encounter with a ghostlike apparition on the castle battlements. "There are more things in heaven and earth," his friend Hamlet assures him, "than are dreamt of in your philosophy."

Many people today would readily agree with Hamlet that the world and the vast universe surrounding it are teeming with wonders and oddities that remain largely outside the realm of present human knowledge or understanding. How did the universe begin? What caused the dinosaurs to become extinct? Was the lost continent of Atlantis a real place or merely legendary? Does a monstrous creature lurk beneath the surface of Scotland's Loch Ness? These are only a few of the intriguing questions that remain unanswered, despite the many great strides made by science in recent centuries.

Lucent Books' Mystery Library series is dedicated to exploring these and other perplexing, sometimes bizarre, and often disturbing or frightening wonders. Each volume in the series presents the best-known tales, incidents, and evidence surrounding the topic in question. Also included are the opinions and theories of scientists and other experts who have attempted to unravel and solve the ongoing mystery. And supplementing this information is a fulsome list of sources for further reading, providing the reader with the means to pursue the topic further.

The Mystery Library will satisfy every young reader's fascination for the unexplained. As one of history's greatest scientists, physicist Albert Einstein, put it:

The most beautiful thing we can experience is the mysterious. It is the source of all true art and science. He to whom this emotion is a stranger, who can no longer wonder and stand rapt in awe, is as good as dead: his eyes are closed.

A Mysterious Disappearance

On May 20, 1937, American aviator Amelia Earhart boarded her plane and lifted off the ground in Oakland, California, first heading south and then east, intending to fly around the world along the equator. If successful, this carefully planned journey would make her the first pilot to circumnavigate the globe by this route. It would require Earhart and her sole crew member, navigator Fred Noonan, to travel thousands of miles and land in cities and towns across the United States, South America, Africa, India, and Australia, and on islands in the Atlantic, Indian, and Pacific oceans.

Such a flight was not only long, it was difficult. Earhart's plane lacked the sophisticated navigation and communication equipment of today's aircraft, so she risked missing her landing sites. In addition, her plane's cockpit was cramped, noisy, and often reeked of gasoline fumes, and its engines and landing gear were unreliable. In fact, Earhart's plane was so plagued with mechanical problems prior to her Oakland takeoff that some of her friends urged her to delay her attempt at circumnavigation.

But Earhart was not to be deterred. She was known for taking risks, and she had already made several record-setting flights.

In 1928 she became the first woman to cross the Atlantic Ocean in an airplane—though as a passenger rather than a pilot. In 1930 she set a women's speed record for a flight of 100 kilometers, going 174.89 miles per hour. In 1932 she became the first woman and just the second pilot ever to complete a solo flight across the Atlantic Ocean. (The first pilot to make this crossing solo was Charles Lindbergh in 1927.) In 1935 Earhart made a solo flight from Hawaii to California along a route that no pilot had ever before taken successfully.

In 1932 Amelia Earhart flew this plane solo across the Atlantic Ocean.

At the urging of her business manager, George Palmer Putnam (who in 1931 also became her husband), Earhart wrote books and gave speeches about her achievements. As a result, she achieved worldwide fame, and her fans often compared her to Lindbergh. In fact, both aviators fit the public's notion of a heroic figure: tall, blond, attractive, adventurous, and charismatic. Even Lindbergh's wife, Anne Morrow Lindbergh, said, "It startles me how much alike they are."[1]

Earhart was not the only female pilot to have set records during the 1930s. For example, in 1931 Ruth Nichols set a record for flying the highest (28,743 feet), fastest (210.63 miles per hour), and farthest in a single flight (1977.6 miles) of any woman pilot. By this time, there were 472 licensed female pilots in the United States, some of whom were reputed to be far more skilled than Earhart. Nonetheless, because of her charisma and Putnam's public relations efforts, Earhart became the best-known female aviator of her time. She also became a leading symbol of the women's rights movement, a position she welcomed. Shortly before her attempt at circumnavigation, she wrote:

> "Because I want to." That was as near a complete reply [to the question, "Why fly around the world?"] as I could devise. Here was shining adventure, beckoning with new experiences, added knowledge of flying, of peoples—of myself. . . .
>
> Then, too, there was my belief that now and then women should do for themselves what men have already done—and occasionally what men have not done—thereby establishing themselves as persons, and perhaps encouraging other women toward greater independence of thought and action. . . .[2]

But in June 1937, Earhart became something else as well: the center of one of the greatest mysteries in American history. Toward the end of her flight around the globe, as she was flying to Howland Island in the Pacific Ocean, her plane disappeared. No sign of the plane, Amelia Earhart, or Fred Noonan was ever found, despite search efforts by both the U.S. government and George Putnam.

So what happened to Amelia Earhart? No one knows, but theories abound. Some say her plane ran out of fuel and crashed into the sea; others say she landed on a Pacific island and died there. Still others believe she survived a crash, either in the ocean or near an island, only to be taken captive by the Japanese and die in their custody. (At that time, just prior to World War II, Japan was aggressively expanding and defending its territory in the Pacific.)

Indeed, in the years following Earhart's disappearance, some radio operators came forward to say they had heard her calling for help after landing, and after World War II some people who had been in the Pacific reported having seen her, her grave, or her plane in what was Japanese-occupied territory at the time of her disappearance. Moreover, in the 1990s a research team studying historical documents concluded that Earhart must have died on a deserted island. Today this group is looking for the wreckage of her plane on that island, but unless hard evidence of her fate is found, Amelia Earhart's disappearance will remain a mystery.

Chapter 1

Who Was Amelia Earhart?

Amelia liked baseball more than frilly dresses but posed here for a formal portrait at age six.

Born on July 24, 1897, in Atchison, Kansas, Amelia Earhart grew up in an environment that contributed to her wanting to become one of the first female aviators. Her childhood was, for the early twentieth century, far more typical of a boy's than a girl's. She climbed fences, played baseball, shot rifles, and, at the age of seven, made a roller coaster out of a cart and a series of wooden boards that ran from a shed roof to the lawn. The first time she tried out her coaster, she careened off the makeshift track and crashed. Unhurt, she was soon back up on the roof to try again—just as in later years she would walk away from plane crashes ready to fly again.

Living in Two Worlds

Amelia had decided to build her roller coaster after seeing one at the World's Fair in St. Louis, Missouri—an expedition that had cost her father, Edwin Earhart, a hundred dollars at a time when he had no money to spare. Irresponsible with money, he often went into debt buying presents for his wife, Amy, and Amelia and her younger sister, Grace Muriel.

Edwin's spending outstripped his income, even though as a lawyer for a railroad company he was well paid.

The Earharts' intermittent poverty frustrated Amelia's mother, who had grown up in a wealthy, socially prominent family. Amy's father, Alfred Otis, was a bank president and retired U.S. District Court judge. Otis complained regularly about his son-in-law's money troubles and looked down on the young man, who was the son of a poor Lutheran minister. Nonetheless, at the time Amy had married Edwin, Otis had bought them a house in Kansas City, Kansas, and furnished it for them. Afterward, he continued to give the couple lavish gifts. Otis was furious when Edwin sold one of them, a set of expensive law books, to pay off a debt.

Amelia was born in her grandparents' house, and she and her sister lived in the Otis home every summer and whenever their parents wanted some time to themselves. During these visits Amelia's grandmother, who was also named Amelia, expected the girls to behave like young ladies. In fact, Grandmother Otis was so strict that she would not allow Amelia to go horseback riding, believing it to be unladylike.

Amelia's parents, however, were much more permissive. In fact, one Christmas, Edwin bought his daughters sleds meant for boys. (Boys' sleds were designed to be ridden downhill while lying down; girls' sleds, in contrast, were designed to be pulled by an adult, with the rider sitting upright.) He also bought them a .22-caliber rifle, which Grandmother Otis later took away from them. Amelia preferred living with her parents and idolized her father; she was largely unaware of her family's money troubles.

New Surroundings

When Amelia was ten, her father made a new home for his family in Des Moines, Iowa, where he had been working for the Rock Island Railroad. Shortly thereafter, the Earharts attended the Iowa State Fair. One of the event's main attractions was an airplane, the first Amelia had ever seen, but

Amelia (center) stands with her parents (right) and sister (left). Although her family sometimes struggled financially, Amelia grew up unaware of any money problems.

she was unimpressed by it. She was too busy studying a souvenir she had just bought: a hat made out of a fruit basket.

Amelia's time in Des Moines was filled with such pleasures. Within a year, her father had gotten a raise in pay, which allowed the family to rent a large house staffed by two servants, to take family vacations, and to enjoy a variety of leisure activities, including attending the theater and art exhibits. During this time, Amelia also learned to ride a horse.

Within four years, however, Amelia's life had lost a lot of its joy. Her father had become an alcoholic, and whenever he was drunk he would verbally abuse his wife and children. Eventually his alcoholism cost him his job, and it took him months to find another.

This new job, a low-paying position as a railway clerk, required the Earhart family to move to St. Paul, Minnesota. There Amelia and her sister attended a public high school and became involved in youth activities at an Episcopal church. Meanwhile, their father continued to drink. Still, he managed to keep his job, and soon he found another one he liked better.

As a result of her father's job-hopping, Amelia changed high schools five times in four years. Later she would credit this experience with making her more flexible than she might otherwise have been. "What we [my sister and I] missed in continuous contacts over a long period," she explained, "we gained by becoming adapted to new surroundings quickly."[3]

Interest in Medicine

In 1916, when Amelia was nineteen, her life changed again. By this time, her grandparents had died, and much of their money had been left to Amelia's mother—but according to Amelia Otis's will, it was to remain in trust, unspent, for twenty years or until after Edwin Earhart's death. Amy Earhart went to court to gain the immediate right to use this money, and when she won the case she paid Amelia's tuition at a private girls' school, the Ogontz School in Rydal, Pennsylvania. There Amelia studied literature, joined a sorority, became active in student politics, and began to show an interest in issues related to women's rights.

After only two years, however, she decided to leave school to become a volunteer nurse's aide at the Spadina Military Hospital in Toronto, Ontario. At the time, Canadian soldiers were fighting in World War I, and Amelia wanted to help with the war effort. She worked primarily in the hospital kitchen, though she also handed out medicine, cleaned up after patients, and performed other menial tasks. During the flu epidemic of 1918, she worked so hard that her own health suffered. She developed an infection that involved her throat, nose, and one eye. In those days antibiotics had not

Although Amelia left Ogontz School before graduating, she appears in a cap and gown in the school's 1917 yearbook.

Amelia Earhart worked as a Canadian nurse's aide during World War I.

yet been discovered, so it took her a long time to recover from this illness.

For a time the young woman drifted. While waiting to regain her strength, Amelia joined her sister in Northampton, Massachusetts. There she took banjo lessons and studied auto mechanics. Eventually, she decided to study medicine. To this end, she enrolled as a premedical student at Columbia University in New York City. After the first year, however, she dropped out and went to live with her parents, who had moved to Southern California.

Flying Lessons

It was in California that Amelia discovered the passion that would last the rest of her life. In December 1920 her father took her to an air show in Long Beach, and afterward she told him that she wanted to go up in a plane. Three days later, he paid for her to take a ride in one at a nearby airfield. She was so exhilarated by the experience that she became determined to take flying lessons. She found a woman pilot in Los Angeles who was willing to teach her; to pay for the lessons Amelia began working for a local telephone company.

Amelia's instructor, Neta Snook, was only a year older than Amelia. The two quickly became friends. At first, Amelia used Neta's plane for her lessons, but she soon borrowed some money from her mother to buy her own. She took possession of this plane, named the *Canary* for its yellow color, on her twenty-fifth birthday, in 1922.

Amelia crashed the *Canary* several times, prompting Cora Kinner, the wife of the airplane's builder, Bert Kinner, to later recall, "She used to scare me to death."[4] Nonetheless, under Neta's guidance, Amelia earned an international pilot's license, the first woman to do so—though, as Amelia later explained, "It wasn't really necessary to have any license at that period. . . . People just flew, when and if they could, in anything which could get off the ground."[5] Neta also taught Amelia how to drive a car, using a borrowed 1921 Model T Ford.

After receiving her pilot's license, Amelia began giving airplane rides to earn gasoline money, supplementing this income

In 1922, Amelia bought this plane, the Canary, *from builder Bert Kinner.*

with other odd jobs. She also attempted to make a name for herself by setting an altitude record at a Los Angeles air show. This record was soon broken by another female aviator, Ruth Nichols, and Amelia nearly crashed trying to top it.

Another Change of Focus

Unfortunately, by this time Amelia's parents had lost all their money, having invested their inheritance on a gypsum mine that was destroyed in a flood. Amelia and her sister tried to help the family stay afloat financially, but eventually their parents divorced, and in the spring of 1924, Amelia sold her plane and moved to Boston, Massachusetts, with her mother and sister to start a new life. (The plane's buyer, a beginning pilot, crashed it on his first flight, killing himself and his passenger.) Amelia returned to Columbia University, but after a year she could no longer afford the tuition, so she dropped out and moved back to Boston, where she took a job teaching English to immigrants. The following year she joined the staff of the Denison House, a facility offering social services to poor immigrants.

By this time, Amelia was flying again. She had convinced Bert Kinner to let her act as his sales representative in the Boston area, in exchange for the use of one of his planes. She also signed up for more flying lessons at a nearby airport. Whenever she was not working at the Denison House she was usually in the air.

As she had in California, Amelia gained notoriety for being one of the few female pilots in her state, and in 1928 she came to the attention of a public relations man, former army captain Hilton H. Railey, who was specifically looking for a female pilot. Railey was working for a group that wanted to sponsor the first flight of a woman across the Atlantic Ocean. These people wanted an experienced pilot, because whomever they chose for their flight had to be unafraid in the air and accustomed to the tight quarters of an airplane cabin. However, the woman would not actually be flying the plane, which was named *Friendship*. Instead, she would be a passenger on the flight—

in keeping with the prevailing belief of those times that no woman could successfully pilot a plane such a distance.

Amelia didn't care for this arrangement, but she wanted to make history. She agreed to meet with her potential sponsors, and when they offered her the flight, she agreed to go, even though, as a passenger, she would not be paid. On June 3, 1928, she boarded the *Friendship* in Boston, and with pilot Wilmer L. Stultz and mechanic and copilot Louis "Slim" Gordon, she flew to Halifax, Nova Scotia. The next day the trio flew to Trepassy, Newfoundland, where they remained for nearly two weeks waiting for favorable weather. They then flew across the Atlantic to the United Kingdom, landing on June 18, 1928, after a flight of twenty hours and forty minutes. Through the entire flight, Amelia had to sit on the floor beside two large gas tanks.

A crowd gathers to watch the Friendship—*with Amelia Earhart, Wilmer L. Stultz, and Louis Gordon aboard— take off in 1928.*

Dealing with Celebrity

Despite Earhart's limited role, the public's response to her flight was immediate. As soon as she landed, crowds gathered to celebrate her becoming the first woman to cross the Atlantic. Reporters swarmed her as well, many of them dubbing her "Lady Lindy" for her resemblance to Charles Lindbergh, who only a year earlier had become the first man to make a solo flight across the Atlantic Ocean. Earhart later learned that this resemblance had been a key factor in her being chosen for the flight; Railey had correctly guessed that the press would compare Earhart with Lindbergh.

Back in the United States, where the *Friendship* had been transported by ship, Earhart and her crewmates were feted with a ticker-tape parade through New York City. They had similar experiences in Chicago and Boston, where nearly three hundred thousand people crowded along the streets to catch a glimpse of Earhart. Afterward, Earhart turned her attention toward her next challenge: writing a book about her experiences.

Amelia Earhart and publisher George Putnam married in February 1931.

One of the organizers of her transatlantic flight had been George Palmer Putnam, the head of the publishing company G.P. Putnam's Sons, founded by his grandfather. This company had published Charles Lindbergh's 1927 book *We*, about his famous flight, and as soon as Earhart agreed to cross the Atlantic, Putnam insisted she sign a contract to write a similar book. Called *20 Hrs., 40 Min.: Our Flight in the Friendship*, this book's 1928 publication added to Earhart's fame, as did the numerous speaking engagements she accepted at Putnam's urging.

Over the next few years, Earhart earned thousands of dollars from the lecture circuit, traveling throughout the country, giving as many as twenty-seven speeches a month. She also wrote a series of articles for *Cosmopolitan* magazine, and she participated in a number of aviation events. For example, in 1929, she competed against eighteen other licensed female pilots in the first all-woman transcontinental aviation race. Called the Women's Air Derby, this competition started in Santa Monica, California, and ended in Cleveland, Ohio; Earhart crossed the finish line in third place. Afterward, she was involved in forming an organization dedicated to women's aviation, the Ninety-Nines—so named because it began with ninety-nine charter members—and became the group's first president.

Mrs. George Putnam

George Putnam, acting as her business manager, looked after Earhart's busy schedule. Putnam had long been drawn to celebrities, enjoying the attention he received when he was with them, and he convinced Earhart to let him manage her affairs. He also started socializing with her, even though he was married and had two children. For a while, his wife—wealthy socialite Dorothy Binney—spent time with Earhart as well. In fact, in July 1929 Earhart vacationed with the Putnam family in Rhode Island. But eventually Putnam left his wife of eighteen years and asked Earhart to marry him. He proposed to her six times before she agreed. However, she insisted on keeping her maiden name, and throughout their marriage she tried to maintain her independence.

Putnam and Earhart were married on February 7, 1931. Shortly thereafter, Putnam left his publishing company in order to spend nearly all of his time promoting his new wife. Soon her name was associated with a brand of luggage, a line

A Reluctance to Marry

A few hours before her wedding to George Putnam, Amelia Earhart handed him a letter explaining her thoughts on their impending marriage. In her letter, which appears in Jean L. Backus's *Letters from Amelia, 1901–1937*, she wrote:

Dear GP,

There are some things which should be writ before we are married. Things we have talked over before—most of them.

You must know again my reluctance to marry, my feeling that I shatter thereby chances in work which means so much to me. I feel the move just now as foolish as anything I could do. I know there may be compensations, but have no heart to look ahead.

In our life together I shall not hold you to any medieval code of faithfulness to me, nor shall I consider myself bound to you similarly. If we can be honest I think the differences which arise may best be avoided.

Please let us not interfere with each other's work or play, nor let the world see private joys or disagreements. In this connection I may have to keep some place where I can go to be myself now and then, for I cannot guarantee to endure at all times the confinements of even an attractive cage.

I must exact a cruel promise, and this is that you will let me go in a year if we find no happiness together.

I will try to do my best in every way.

A.E.

of women's clothing, and other products. She also participated in various events to promote aviation—and herself. For example, she became the first woman to fly alone in an autogiro, the forerunner to the helicopter. During a subsequent three-hour flight, she set an autogiro altitude record of 18,415 feet, and the manufacturer of the craft hired her to travel to various cities to demonstrate autogiro flying.

More Aviation Records

Despite such successes, however, Earhart felt that she had not really earned her fame, because she had been only a passenger during the *Friendship*'s transatlantic flight. As she later wrote, "To me, it was genuinely surprising what a disproportion of attention was given to the woman member of the *Friendship* crew at the expense of the men, who were really responsible for the flight."[6]

Consequently, in 1932 she decided to recreate the voyage, this time as the plane's pilot.

Earhart, however, decided to make the flight alone. Although Lindbergh had done this, none of the eight pilots who had crossed the Atlantic in the five years since his flight had done so without a crew; the two who had tried flying solo had disappeared. Earhart, if she succeeded, would be the first woman to make the flight solo. Moreover, she was determined to prove herself as good a pilot as any man. So it was that on May 20, she flew solo out of Newfoundland in her own Vega airplane, headed across the ocean, and landed in southern Ireland just fourteen hours and fifty-six minutes later, despite encountering a severe storm and thick fog.

In 1931, Amelia Earhart flew this autogiro to a height of 18,415 feet and set an altitude record.

President Herbert Hoover presents Amelia Earhart with one of several medals she received commemorating her transatlantic flight.

Now Earhart was feted all over again, both in Europe and in the United States. She rode in parades, received medals of honor, and met dignitaries, including Britain's prince of Wales, the king of Belgium, and U.S. president Herbert Hoover. This time, Earhart felt she deserved the recognition, and she wanted more. As her sister later explained:

> Amelia's position at the pinnacle of aviation fame [after her solo transatlantic flight] demanded that she

follow one of two courses: either vanish into semi-retirement as Colonel Lindbergh chose to do, or else accept the challenge of making more pioneering flights in the as-yet-unexplored skyways. Amelia, if not actually urged by [George Putnam], certainly abetted by him, chose the latter course.[7]

More Self-Promotion

When Earhart was planning her Atlantic crossing, Putnam had encouraged her to start writing *The Fun of It*, another book about her aviation experiences. With the addition of a final chapter on her latest exploit, it was published shortly after her flight to capitalize on her success. In the book, Earhart said the title summarized her motivation for undertaking the flight. However, to a friend she revealed that her motivation was primarily financial, saying, "It's a routine. . . . I make a record and then I lecture on it. That's where the money comes from. Until it's time to make another record."[8]

Lady Lindy

Because Amelia Earhart bore a strong resemblance to American aviator Charles Lindbergh, promoter George Putnam encouraged the press to call Earhart "Lady Lindy." As A. Scott Berg explains in his biography *Lindbergh*, America worshipped Lindbergh with "ceaseless adoration," and after the aviator's 1927 solo flight across the Atlantic,

Lindbergh's fame kept spreading, etching itself deeper into the public consciousness. He was, parents explained to their children, "living history"; and a worshipful nation paid homage and tribute. Official gifts and citations were presented wherever he stopped. . . . Lindbergh began to appear in textbooks; schoolchildren wrote essays on him and dedicated their yearbooks to him; and many schools were named for him. . . . Mountains, lakes, parks, boulevards, islands, bays, and beaches across America and beyond were renamed in his honor.

For his part, Lindbergh himself thought little of Earhart's aviation skills. According to Berg, on one occasion Lindberg joked that he had "heard Amelia made a very good landing—once."

After her transatlantic flight, Earhart embarked on a series of attempts to set records. In July 1932 she tried to fly non-stop across the country; though she was forced to land briefly in Columbus, Ohio, to fix a damaged fuel line, she still set a women's speed record for transcontinental flight, traveling from California to New York in nineteen hours, fourteen minutes. (Had she not stopped en route, she might have beaten the men's record of seventeen hours, thirty-eight minutes.) The following month, Earhart again tried a solo nonstop transcontinental flight. She not only succeeded, with a time of nineteen hours and five minutes, but set a women's distance record of 2,447 miles. A year later, in July 1933, she flew across the country in seventeen hours and seven minutes, beating her own record for a women's solo transcontinental flight.

Afterward, Putnam insisted that his wife concentrate on self-promotion for a while, and she spent the next two years giving speeches and making public appearances. By late 1934, however, the two felt it was time for Earhart to try another publicity-generating flight. After careful planning, in January 1935 she became the first woman to pilot a plane from Hawaii to California. She had planned to refuel in California and continue on to Washington, D.C., hoping to establish another women's distance record and perhaps a speed record as well, but bad weather prevented the transcontinental part of her journey. Still, her accomplishment was monumental. Many other aviators had died trying to make the same Pacific crossing.

The public's response to Earhart's flight was as enthusiastic as ever; crowds gathered to cheer her when she landed in California. The media, however, had become more cynical about her exploits. For example, *Newsweek* magazine wrote, "Every so often Miss Earhart, like other prominent flyers, pulls a spectacular stunt to hit the front pages [of the newspaper]. This enhances a flyer's value as a . . . [product] endorser, helps finance new planes, sometimes publicizes a book."[9]

Nonetheless, Earhart tackled another aviation challenge a few months later. In May 1935 she became the first person to fly nonstop from Mexico City to New Jersey, making the journey in fourteen hours and eighteen minutes. She then hit the lecture circuit again, making more than 130 speeches before the year was over. She also ordered a new airplane, which she intended to fly around the world in yet another attempt to make history. Unfortunately, this adventure would be her last.

Enthusiastic crowds like this one greeted Earhart on her return home following her transatlantic flight.

Chapter 2

A Plan to Circle the Globe

A melia Earhart was one of the most recognized women in the world, but by the fall of 1935, other female pilots were challenging Earhart's prominence in aviation. For example, in September 1935 Beryl Markham successfully flew solo across the Atlantic, but whereas Earhart had flown the route from west to east, Markham was the first woman to make it from east to west. Some people speculated that Earhart might try to do the same, but she did not want to duplicate someone else's success. Instead she planned to fly around the world from east to west, starting from California, in order to keep her place as America's top female aviator.

In and of itself, circumnavigating the globe in an airplane would not be a first. Several other aviators had already accomplished this feat; in fact, Wiley Post had done it twice, in 1931 with a crew member and in 1933 alone. However, none of these pilots had remained close to the equator for the entire journey as Earhart intended, which would make her the first person to take the longest possible route around the world.

The Electra

In order to fly around the world, though, Earhart needed a new airplane, and she could not afford one suitable for such a long-distance flight. Consequently George Putnam sought financial assistance from Purdue University in Lafayette, Indiana. Purdue was one of the few universities in the world with studies in aviation and had hired Earhart as a visiting faculty member. Putnam told the university that Earhart needed the new plane in order to conduct research flights that would "test some of the human reactions to flying-reactions involving diet and altitude, fatigue, the effect of stratosphere flying on creatures conditioned

Earhart's Records

Prior to her around-the-world flight, Earhart set a number of aviation records, including the following:

Year	Location	Type of Record
1922	Long Beach, CA	Altitude (14,000 feet)
1928	Atlantic Ocean	First woman to cross Atlantic by air
1928	American continent	First woman solo transcontinental round-trip
1930	Detroit, MI	Speed record for distance of 100 km (174.89 miles per hour)
1931	Willow Grove, PA	Altitude in autogiro (18,415 feet)
1932	Atlantic Ocean	First woman to cross Atlantic solo
1932	Atlantic Ocean	First woman to cross Atlantic twice
1932	American continent	Women's transcontinental speed record, made west to east (19 hours, 5 minutes)
1933	American continent	Women's transcontinental speed record, made west to east (17 hours, 7 minutes)
1935	Pacific Ocean	First pilot to successfully complete Hawaii–California flight, and first to fly solo across the Pacific
1935	U.S./Mexico	First pilot to fly solo from Los Angeles to Mexico City and from Mexico to New Jersey
1937	Pacific Ocean	Speed record for flight from Oakland, California, to Honolulu, Hawaii (15 hours, 52 minutes)

to the dense air of lower altitude, difference between the reactions of men and women to air travel, if any."[10]

After some persuasion, the university gave Earhart fifty thousand dollars to use for aviation research purposes. Though this was only about half of what Putnam would eventually need to buy and equip a plane for a long-distance flight (the remainder would come from other donors and publicity events), it was enough for Putnam to start shopping for a suitable aircraft. Since much of the trip would be over open ocean, he considered purchasing a seaplane, which could be landed on water. Putnam approached an airplane company, Lockheed, about putting pontoons on one of its ten-passenger commercial planes, the Electra 10. But when Lockheed offered him a smaller Electra, the Model 10E Special, with retractable wheels, Putnam agreed. Unburdened by bulky pontoons, this aircraft would consume less fuel than a seaplane would. Only partially built, this all-metal twin-engine plane could be modified according to Earhart's needs.

George Putnam acquired this plane, the Lockheed Electra 10E Special, for his wife's trip around the world.

Air Races

Amelia Earhart competed in air races, including the 1929 National Air Races, at which she helped create a women's aviation group known as the Ninety-Nines. Such events were extremely popular, but they also served a greater purpose: helping to advance aviation technology by calling attention to pilots' needs. As historian Roger E. Bilstein explains in *Flight in America, 1900–1983:*

> In headlines and crowds, the men and women who flew the planes received the sort of acclaim granted to astronauts a generation later. Among other things, the air races presumably contributed to improved fuels and better engines. But racing planes were highly specialized, with designs not always suitable for agile combat planes or reliable, economical airliners. They were also dangerous. All seven models of the . . . Gee Bee racers of the early thirties crashed, killing five pilots. Some knowledgeable experts looked askance at the continual tinkering with finely tuned engines that required carefully concocted formulas for fuel; skeptical engineers saw no fundamental contributions to flight technology. On the other hand, the air races brought attention to certain mechanical accessories, like retractable landing gear. The striking, long-range efforts of the decade highlighted enhanced reliability in aeronautics and focused attention on time/distance factors for national and international geography alike.

Amelia Earhart (fourth from right) poses with other women aviators who took part in the 1929 Women's Air Derby.

Putnam took possession of the plane in March 1936 and immediately arranged for the necessary modifications, in consultation with Earhart's technical adviser, Paul Mantz. A movie, stunt, and charter pilot with many years of experience, Mantz had helped Earhart with preparations for her Hawaii-to-California flight the previous year. It was Mantz who determined how much fuel the Electra should hold, given that Earhart would be flying long stretches over the Pacific Ocean.

Earhart tests the Westinghouse radio in her Electra.

Plane Modifications

The Electra came with two 81-gallon fuel tanks and two 44-gallon fuel tanks; Mantz had them replaced with two 102-gallon tanks and added another 81-gallon tank, two 132-gallon tanks, and three 153-gallon tanks. In all, then, Earhart's Electra could carry 1,170 gallons of fuel, which, by some estimates, would allow her to remain in the air for twenty-four hours straight. After some argument, Mantz also convinced Putnam to install a Sperry Robot, an autopiloting device that would keep the aircraft flying steady when Earhart could not be at the controls. This equipment was necessary, given the fuel system that Mantz had devised. Most of the Electra's fuel would be in tanks located in the passenger compartment of the plane, but there was no direct line from these to the engines. To transfer fuel from these tanks to those fueling her engines, Earhart would have to leave the cockpit to operate a manual pump.

In addition to the Sperry Robot pilot, Mantz insisted that Earhart's plane carry a Western Electric radio that could broadcast either the human voice or Morse code on all available frequencies. He also made sure her plane had a special rear hatch that would allow a navigator to look up into the sky to see the position of the stars. However, Mantz could not convince Putnam to install an intercom that would allow Earhart to communicate easily with her navigator, who, because of the passenger-compartment fuel tanks, would be trapped in the back of the plane. Instead she planned to rely on a more primitive system whereby pilot and navigator passed notes back and forth over the tanks by clipping their communications to the end of a bamboo pole.

Choosing a Navigator

Earhart had always planned to take a navigator along on her flight, because she had no experience with celestial navigation and extremely limited experience with radio navigation. Previously she had relied primarily on visual sightings of land, combined with luck, to keep her from getting lost, but even then she sometimes put down her plane a few hundred miles from the intended landing site. In fact, during her solo flight across the Atlantic, she had meant to land in Paris, France, but instead ended up in Ireland. This type of error would be disastrous on a flight across the Pacific Ocean, where she had to locate landing sites on islands. Also, because she did not know Morse code, she wanted a navigator who was familiar with this system of communication.

Earhart set out to find a navigator who had the skills she lacked. One such man was Bradford Washburn, a pilot and explorer who was experienced at navigating by the stars. During his interview with Earhart, however, Washburn pointed out some flaws in Earhart's plans. He later wrote:

> Her plan all seemed to make reasonable good sense to me except for her plan for navigation between Darwin, Australia, and Howland Island. . . . I asked her how she planned to hit Howland at the end of a 2,000-mile flight *without a single intermediate emergency-landing spot.* She simply replied: Dead reckoning [i.e., following precalculated compass headings] and star-and-sun sights. Howland Island, as I remember it, is a sliver of land in an immense mass of trackless ocean—about a mile and a half long and a half-mile wide. . . .
>
> I'd made a number of flights in the [type of] Lockheed Electra that she planned to use. . . . I pointed out that, as I recollected it, this airplane cruised most economically at about 9,000 feet. . . . This would seem to give visibility over a reasonably wide sweep of ocean—*if it was cloudless.* But even in excellent weather, I pointed out, the Pacific rapidly develops an intricate pattern of . . . clouds almost every morning, as soon as the sun rises high enough to heat the surface of the ocean. This would make it extremely difficult (if not impossible) to see a small island from 9–12,000 feet in the air. It would either be obscured by the clouds, or badly confused with cloud-shadows which are usually very convincing "islands" until you approach them closely.[11]

Washburn suggested that Putnam have a radio transmitter installed on Howland Island and a corresponding receiver, the radio direction finder, installed on her plane; through a process of transmitting and receiving sounds, this equipment would direct Earhart to the landing site. Instead, Earhart and

Putnam chose a different navigator, though later they would add radio direction-finding equipment to their plane. Their selection was Capt. Harry Manning, who had been the navigator on the ship that had carried the *Friendship* back to the United States after Earhart's Atlantic crossing as a passenger.

Manning was experienced in celestial navigation, and he knew Morse code. Moreover, he was able to take a six-month leave from his job in order to work with Earhart. However, he had no experience in aerial navigation, and as the

Earhart chose (from left) Paul Mantz, Harry Manning, and Fred Noonan to be navigators on her trip around the world.

flight grew closer, Earhart became worried about his ability to find Howland Island. Consequently she decided to test his aerial navigation skills—and the results were disappointing. In his book *Amelia Earhart: The Final Story,* Vincent Loomis reports:

> Amelia . . . took Manning out over the Pacific in the Electra and asked him to chart a course back to Los Angeles. What actually happened depends upon which of the two stories is accurate. Amelia said the captain miscalculated by 200 miles. Manning said it was Amelia who was off course, and that she tended to drift to the left consistently when trying to follow a heading. Regardless, both sides agreed an assistant navigator would be a wise precaution, at least for the . . . Pacific legs [of the flight].[12]

Fred Noonan

In March 1937, the same month she was planning to make her circumnavigation attempt, Earhart chose forty-four-year-old Fred Noonan as assistant navigator. Noonan had learned navigation as a sailor on a variety of ships (he first went to sea at age fifteen) and after World War I he became both a pilot and an aerial navigator. Noonan worked for a major airline, Pan Am Airways, from September 1930 to January 1937. During this period, he not only piloted planes but taught navigation, inspected airports, and was the navigator for a series of survey flights across the Pacific Ocean. One of Noonan's coworkers, Victor A. Wright, later said:

> [The] success of these early survey flights was due to a large extent to Fred Noonan's development of aerial navigation techniques, for . . . there was no one else available who had the imagination and the ability to carry out this trying and exacting work of navigation in a new element. The radio beacons were useful up

to certain distances offshore, but there were some long, lonely stretches in between where the only thing we had to depend on was Fred's ability as a navigator.[13]

When he met Earhart, Noonan had recently left his Pan Am job, supposedly because he felt that the job no longer offered him enough challenges or chances for promotion. However, there were rumors that he had been quietly asked to leave Pan Am because of alcoholism. According to Wright, Noonan never drank while on duty, but Loomis reports:

Pilots who flew with Noonan on the San Francisco-to-Hawaii route . . . [said] that Fred's procedure was to set up his charts at the beginning of the flight and then retire to the lavatory with his briefcase. Later, after doing some work at the navigation table for an hour or so, he would again disappear. Finally, after this routine had been repeated several times, he would have to be guided to a bunk to sleep off his [alcoholic] stupor while the rest of the crew filled in for him.[14]

Earhart had apparently heard the rumors about Noonan's alcoholism, but she seemed unconcerned. She did not plan to have alcohol aboard her plane, and Noonan was by all accounts an excellent navigator when sober. In addition, he would not be the only navigator aboard, and he would participate only in the Pacific legs of the journey, where his experience would be invaluable. Furthermore, Earhart planned to tackle this leg of her journey first; afterward she would drop Noonan off in Australia and continue on with Manning. At this point, Earhart was thinking of dropping Manning off as well, sometime later in the flight, because Putnam thought it would be better publicity for her to end her circumnavigation alone. But Paul Mantz thought that it was foolish for Earhart to consider flying solo. He had noticed that she became easily fatigued while flying, and that this fatigue sometimes affected her ability to handle the airplane.

Noonan and Earhart study the map of their planned route.

For example, during one test flight of the Electra, Earhart was so drained after just an eighty-mile flight that she asked Mantz to land the plane for her. Moreover, when subjected to enough stress, Earhart developed one illness or another—and her circumnavigation was definitely stressful enough and long enough for Earhart to become sick. If she did, pilot error would be even more likely.

A False Start

In fact, pilot error might have been a factor in a runway accident that occurred when Earhart finally began her attempt at circumnavigation. On March 17, 1937, she began her long journey by flying from California to Hawaii. The trip took only fifteen hours and forty-seven minutes, a new record for the route. Afterward she planned to rest just eight hours before taking off on the next leg of her circumnavigation. However, bad weather delayed her departure until 7:35 A.M. on March 20. Then, when she tried to take off on the eighteen-hundred-mile leg to Howland Island, something went wrong. According to witnesses, her wing dipped, the plane slid right, and the right landing gear ripped off. Gasoline leaked onto the runway, and Earhart quickly cut her engines, fearing her plane would burst into flames.

Aviation experts disagreed about what caused Earhart's mishap. Some blamed runway conditions, since a few spots were slick with rain. Others blamed a blown tire, because after the accident the right tire was found to be flat. Others

Amelia Earhart inspects her damaged plane after an accident in Hawaii.

cited the plane's landing gear—and indeed ten weeks later this gear did malfunction on another runway. Still others blamed the plane's load of fuel, saying that if Earhart's tanks were not full enough, the gasoline had room to slosh violently back and forth—a motion that might have forced the craft to veer off course.

Mantz, however, blamed Earhart. Though she herself never admitted publicly to being at fault, Mantz said later that in trying to take off, she had one engine running faster than the other, something he had warned her to avoid. A few others on the scene shared this view. Lt. William C. Capp, an army air corps officer who had witnessed the takeoff, also blamed Earhart, and he later became one of her greatest critics. According to biographer Doris Rich in her book *Amelia Earhart: A Biography:*

> Capp said she was an inept pilot who would not take the advice of experts. . . . Capp did allow for several possibilities that might have made the takeoff more difficult. There could have been a cross wind or unusual wind currents, or a sloppily loaded plane. There was also a peculiar arrangement of buildings at the end of the runway, he said, which created a threatening illusion similar to that of sailing under a bridge. But basically Capp thought that Amelia was not a good pilot.[15]

Another Try

To silence her critics, Earhart was eager to make another try at circumnavigation, but first she had to get her plane repaired. Not only the landing gear but the propellers and right wing were damaged, and it would cost more than twenty-five thousand dollars to fix them. To cover this expense, Putnam had to find more donors and Earhart had to make more public appearances. In addition, Earhart would carry stamped envelopes on her flight to sell afterwards as souvenirs.

Earhart's fund-raising activities worried Mantz, because they were keeping Earhart away from the Electra. Mantz felt that during the three months it would take to ready the plane for another around-the-world flight, Earhart should be practicing, familiarizing herself with the plane and its equipment, particularly the radio. Manning was also disappointed with Earhart's behavior, and eventually he decided that he no longer wanted to be her navigator. Earhart told the press that Manning had backed out of the trip because his leave of absence from his job was about to end. Much later, however, Manning said:

> Amelia was responsible for the crash [in Hawaii] . . . overcorrected to the left, then to the right, gas leaking, sparks. We were all just . . . lucky it didn't catch fire. [Amelia] was something of a prima donna—had an ego and could be tough as nails. I got very fed up with her bull-headedness several times. That's why she brought Noonan into the picture—in the event that I gave up on the flight.[16]

Another aspect of Earhart's plans also changed during this period. While her plane was being repaired, she decided to reverse the direction of her flight, putting the Pacific Ocean crossing at the end.

Earhart's participation in moneymaking promotions like this one for Lucky Strike cigarettes cut into her practice time.

Amelia M. Earhart, first woman to fly the Atlantic by aeroplane

says—

"Lucky Strikes were the cigarettes carried on the 'Friendship' when she crossed the Atlantic. They were smoked continuously from Trepassey to Wales. I think nothing else helped so much to lessen the strain for all of us."

"It's toasted"

No Throat Irritation-No Cough.

© 1928 The American Tobacco Co., Manufacturer

Of this decision she wrote, "A compelling factor in our decision was the probable imminence in the Caribbean and African areas of much less favorable weather later than early June. So it seemed sensible to get this part of the journey over as promptly as possible."[17]

However, this meant that the most difficult leg of the trip, from Honolulu to Howland Island, would come near the end, when Earhart was likely to be exhausted. It also meant that Noonan would have to accompany Earhart on the entire flight. More importantly, because of the earth's rotation, if Earhart flew east she would lose an hour of daylight for every nine hundred nautical miles. (Flying west, she would gain an hour instead.)

Consequently some people advised Earhart to wait to make her trip until the following year, so that she could fly it from west to east as originally planned. She ignored this advice. Moreover, she removed the Morse code key from her plane's radio, since Noonan was not good at operating it. However, she kept the equipment that allowed her to cable reports of her journey to the *New York Tribune* newspaper, as part of a deal arranged by Putnam.

Government Paperwork

Putnam handled all publicity related to Earhart's trip, as well as all government paperwork—not only from the United States but from foreign countries that required aviators to receive official permissions to fly over their land. These permissions were sometimes difficult to obtain. As Earhart explained:

> In addition to routine passports and visas, in much of the territory it was necessary to secure special authority to land a plane. Here and there were forbidden regions over which one might not fly. In and over other territories no firearms or motion picture cameras were permitted. Medical credentials were necessary; pilot

and navigator were swollen with a full personal cargo of vaccines and inoculations. A couple of countries required testimonial of character and a negative police record. These I contrived.[18]

Putnam also had to coordinate Earhart's movements with the U.S. government, because some of Earhart's landing sites were on military bases. In addition, the U.S. Navy was planning to station at least one ship off of Howland Island to provide Earhart with radio guidance, fuel, and emergency services if necessary. Pan Am Airways also offered to help Earhart by equipping her radio with a transmitting device that would

The night before her departure, Amelia Earhart and George Putnam study the route Earhart will take on her planned flight around the world.

enable the airline to track her movements across the Pacific in case she needed to be rescued. She refused the offer.

Then, with no fanfare, she was on her way. Telling everyone but her husband and crew that she was merely testing her newly repaired plane, she flew from Oakland, California, to Miami, Florida, on May 21, 1937; this was the first leg of her eastward flight around the world. Accompanying her were Fred Noonan, George Putnam, and her mechanic, Bo McKneely. Only Earhart and Noonan, however, would be making the leg of the trip that would land on Howland Island. That flight would be the last adventure either would ever have.

Chapter 3

A Doomed Flight

Before Amelia Earhart left Oakland, California, for her flight around the world, she was supposed to meet with Paul Mantz to go over her flight plans and fuel-consumption estimates and to perform last-minute checkups of her equipment. Instead, she left a few days ahead of schedule, on May 21, 1937, while Mantz was out of town. Earhart supposedly did this to prevent reporters from bothering her as she tried to take off. Mantz, however, felt that Earhart was avoiding him.

Mantz's opinion was that Earhart was not ready for such a difficult flight. Mantz later said that by evading her pre-flight meeting with him, Earhart had turned his work into "a waste of time, because of her sneak departure" and would consequently be "flying by guesswork."[19]

Tampering with Her Radio

Indeed, a minor catastrophe occurred as soon as Earhart landed at her first stop. Shortly after the plane touched down in Tucson, Arizona, one of its engines burst into flames. These were quickly extinguished, and, Earhart's mechanic, Bo Mc-Kneely, made the necessary repairs, and the next day Earhart,

A successful takeoff in Oakland, California, marks the beginning of Earhart's around-the-world journey.

Noonan, McKneely, and Putnam took off again, even though a sandstorm was raging.

Earhart's next stop was Miami, Florida, where she stayed for nine days. During this period, she got rid of an extra radio antenna Mantz had installed to allow her to transmit on a frequency of 500 kilocycles. Earhart had never wanted this 250-foot antenna, known as a trailing wire, for two reasons. First, it was cumbersome to use; stored on a spool inside the plane, it had to be played out after takeoff and reeled in before a landing. Second, the mechanism that turned the spool was heavy, and for maximum fuel efficiency her airplane needed to be as light as possible.

Consequently, Earhart eagerly accepted the advice of a Miami radioman who said that if she made certain changes to her standard antenna, she could remove the trailing wire and still be able to receive messages on 500, though she would only be able to transmit on higher frequencies. However, as Bradford Washburn later reported, sending messages on these higher frequencies would have "vastly reduced the number of people who might conceivably pick her up."[20]

Moreover, most radio direction finders were unable to home in on higher frequencies. The most reliable and widely used radio frequency for naval direction finders was 500—the frequency at which Earhart could no longer transmit signals. In addition, 500 was the standard frequency used for distress calls, so it was monitored constantly by ships at sea. Why Earhart decided to forgo this precaution is a mystery. One possibility is that since distress calls on 500 were always made in Morse code, and neither Earhart nor Noonan were versed in Morse code, Earhart thought the trailing wire pointless.

Radio Direction Finding

Tampering with her radio exposed Earhart to grave risk. In his book *Amelia Earhart's Shoes: Is the Mystery Solved?* Thomas King reports,

> Neither Earhart nor Noonan labored under any illusion that dead reckoning and celestial techniques alone would be sufficient to find Howland Island within the time constraints imposed by their fuel reserves. Unless they were phenomenally lucky, help from the plane's radios would be essential to successfully complete the flight.[21]

King's explanation of how direction finding works shows why it was so risky for Earhart to disable her radio's ability to transmit on 500 kilocycles.

A New Reliance on Instruments

When Earhart first learned to fly, pilots depended on common sense and visual cues to decide when and in which direction to fly. As a result of advances in technology, by the early 1930s many pilots, including Earhart, were increasingly relying on instruments over common sense. Consequently, according to historian Roger E. Bilstein, old-fashioned pilots began to grumble that experience and individual judgment were losing their value. Bilstein reports:

> One Boeing Air Transport pilot, a veteran of early army and air-mail flying, admitted that he liked flying too much to quit, although he felt that the profession had certainly changed. . . . Gone was the time when the pilot was his own commander, basing all decisions on individual judgment. He now got weather advice from a battery of meteorologists, instruction from the ground by radiophone, and flew a course by radio signal which led him safely to lighted airfields. A bit wistfully, the old pilot [said], "all these improvements and safety measures have taken most of the adventure out of the business."

In principle, [radio direction finding] was a bit like finding someone you can't see by having them shout and noting the direction the sound comes from, except this was done with radio waves instead of sound waves. . . . [The] airplane would send out a signal (shout) and the ground station would note the direction the signal came from and tell the pilot which way to fly. The technique could also be reversed, in which case the ground station would send a signal (shout) and the pilot would determine what direction it was coming from. . . . Either way, the pilot would know what compass heading to follow to reach the intended destination.[22]

By removing the trailing wire, then, Earhart had essentially cut her radio's effectiveness in half.

Flying to Africa

Having lightened their load by jettisoning the trailing wire, on June 1 Earhart and Noonan flew from Miami to San Juan, Puerto Rico. They then traveled to Caripito, Venezuela; Paramaibo, Dutch Guiana (now Suriname); Fortazela, Brazil; and Natal, Brazil. From Brazil they flew across the Atlantic Ocean to Africa, where they planned to land in Dakar, French West Africa (now Senegal), on June 7.

When they reached Africa's east coast, however, Earhart's difficulty following her plotted course became apparent. She accidentally hit the African coast north of where she had planned. When she realized that she had missed Dakar, she had to search for a place to land before dark. Turning left and continuing north up the African coast, she eventually found a landing site in St. Louis, a town about 160 miles north of Dakar. The next day she flew south to Dakar, where she waited out a storm.

During a stopover in Hawaii, Earhart and others inspect her radio. On an earlier stop she had removed the radio's extra antenna.

While she waited for the weather to improve, Earhart had her plane checked by mechanics. She was having trouble with her fuel-flow meter that often left her unable to tell how much fuel was left in a particular tank. The mechanics were unable to solve the problem; eventually she started relying on an alarm clock to remind her to switch from one tank to another.

Poor Conditions

On June 10 Earhart and Noonan took off again, and over the next few days they traveled through bad weather, strong winds, and sometimes blistering heat across Africa, the Red Sea, Arabia, Pakistan, and India. By June 19 they had reached Rangoon, Burma; the next day, Singapore; and the next day, Bandoeng, Java (now Bandung, Indonesia). To this point, Earhart had flown more than twenty thousand miles in approximately 135 hours, stopping thirty times along the way.

Many of the stopovers Earhart made were in places where bad food and poor sleeping accommodations were the norm.

Amelia Earhart and Frederick Noonan (left) lunch in Venezuala, one of several stops around the globe.

Consequently, for much of her trip, Earhart suffered from an upset stomach and slept little. Earhart decided to remain in Java for six days, both to recover her strength and to have her plane checked again.

Earhart and Noonan then flew to Timor Island, followed by Darwin, Australia, and Lae, New Guinea. It was at Lae that Earhart received a message from George Putnam saying that he wanted her to land back in Oakland, California, on July 4. Putnam wanted Earhart's successful completion of the journey to coincide with Independence Day, and he had lucrative publicity events scheduled for the days following the American holiday.

Worrisome Problems

Earhart responded to Putnam's message with a cryptic note, saying she would have to stay in Lae a while to deal with radio difficulties and personnel problems. In regard to the latter, she might have been referring to Noonan's alcoholism, since a few people who saw him in New Guinea later reported that he was drinking. However, Earhart might also have been referring to herself, because she was still suffering from fatigue and stomach upsets. In either case, she asked Harry Balfour, a radio operator who worked for New Guinea Airways in Lae, to accompany her and Noonan on their flight to Howland Island to help with navigation. Balfour refused, however.

Earhart had another concern, which was that Noonan's navigational instruments had not been working well. Specifically, his chronometers and a gyroscope were being affected by the airplane's constant heavy vibrations. There was another cause for concern, though neither Earhart nor Noonan was aware of the problem. Noonan's navigational charts were faulty. These charts showed Howland Island to be seven miles to the northwest of its actual location—a fact determined by navigational experts just a year earlier but not widely known.

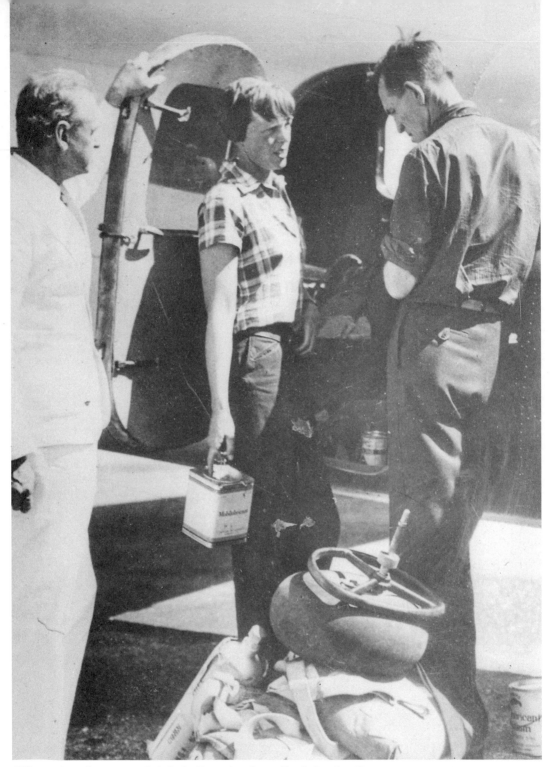

Pilot and navigator stop briefly in Darwin, Australia, before heading on to New Guinea.

Last Preparations

To Earhart, the biggest immediate concern was the weight of her plane. Lae's runway was a crude, short stretch of dirt that ended at a cliff overlooking the ocean, and she was afraid that her craft was so heavy that it would simply drop off the cliff and crash into the ocean. To avoid this she decided to remove some of her supplies. Harry Balfour later reported that this included survival equipment: a life raft, a flare pistol for signaling rescuers, and two parachutes.

By this time, the U.S. Coast Guard had positioned three ships, the *Swan*, the *Ontario*, and the *Itasca*, along her intended route to Howland, as part of a communication system intended to help her navigate to the island. (The *Swan* was between Honolulu and Howland, the *Ontario* halfway between Lae and Howland, and the *Itasca* at Howland.) The *Ontario* had no high-frequency equipment on board, which meant its radio could receive her transmissions only at frequencies of 195 to 600 kilocycles. The other two ships could receive and/or transmit code and voice messages on a variety of frequencies.

Prior to leaving New Guinea, Earhart had exchanged numerous telegrams with the U.S. Coast Guard regarding which radio frequencies she would use to contact these ships. She also set a schedule for these transmissions, so that radio operators would be listening for her at the correct times. In general, Earhart was planning to send voice messages on 6210 kilocycles during the day and 3105 during the night, fifteen minutes before and fifteen minutes after each hour, using Greenwich Civil Time (GCT) as her time zone. On the hour and on the half-hour, the *Itasca* was supposed to send weather reports on those frequencies. In addition, Earhart told the *Itasca* that she would be sending the ship a homing signal on 7500 kilocycles. She asked the Coast Guard to make sure her messages were sent in English, not Morse code, but never made the reason for this request clear.

While in Lae, Earhart received a cable from the *Itasca* saying, in part: *Itasca* transmitters calibrated 7500 6210 3105 500 425 KCS . . . "*Itasca* direction finder frequency range 550 to 270 KCS."[23]

In other words, whereas the *Itasca* would be able to receive Earhart on both high and low frequencies, its direction-finder equipment could pinpoint her location only if she transmitted on a frequency lower than 550. In a previous cable, Earhart had said that she could receive messages from the *Ontario* on 500, so the *Itasca* assumed that Earhart could send messages on this frequency as well. She never told them that by removing the trailing wire from her antenna, she had eliminated this option.

Leaving for Howland

On July 2 Earhart and Noonan were finally ready to leave Lae for Howland Island (where it was then July 1, because the island was on the other side of the international date line). According to personnel at the Lae runway, when the Electra lifted off, it was carrying 1,100 gallons of fuel. This figure is in dispute; some aviation experts estimate that the Electra was carrying somewhere between 980 and 1,016 gallons. Any more fuel than that, these experts say, would have made the plane too heavy to take off. In any case, observers noted that the airplane had trouble lifting off the ground.

Once the Electra was airborne, Earhart turned toward Howland Island. The time of takeoff was noted as exactly 10:00 A.M. local time, or 0000 GCT. A few hours later, at 0418 GCT, Harry Balfour received a message from Earhart on a radio frequency of 6210. Earhart reported that she was flying at an altitude of seven thousand feet and a speed of 140 knots, or more than 150 miles an hour.

At 0519 GCT she reported her altitude as ten thousand feet, and her position indicated that she was on a direct course to Howland Island. At 0718 GCT, she was at eight thousand

feet, at a position roughly 850 miles from Lae and still on course for Howland Island. By this time, however, she had encountered strong headwinds, which—combined with her high altitudes—would reduce the Electra's fuel efficiency. Earhart was nearing the "point of no return," when she would not have enough fuel to turn back to Lae if she decided she could not make it to Howland Island.

Crew members of the USS Itasca *on Howland Island make preparations to support Earhart's landing.*

Past the Point of No Return

Still, Earhart kept going. But at 0815 GCT, when she was scheduled to report her position again, Balfour heard nothing. At around 1030 GCT, though, a radio operator on nearby Nauru Island heard her say, "A ship in sight ahead."[24] What ship this was is still being debated. Some people believe it was a New Zealand cargo ship, the SS *Myrtlebank*, but most

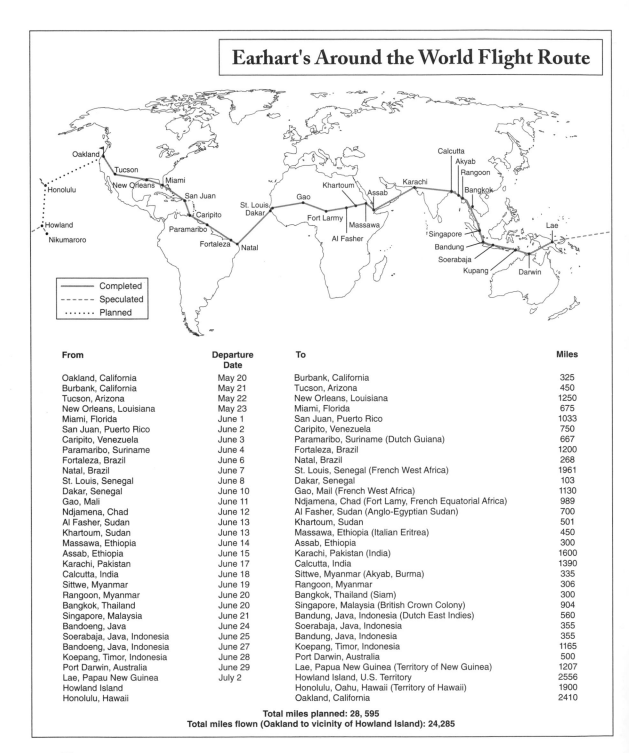

Earhart's Around the World Flight Route

From	Departure Date	To	Miles
Oakland, California	May 20	Burbank, California	325
Burbank, California	May 21	Tucson, Arizona	450
Tucson, Arizona	May 22	New Orleans, Louisiana	1250
New Orleans, Louisiana	May 23	Miami, Florida	675
Miami, Florida	June 1	San Juan, Puerto Rico	1033
San Juan, Puerto Rico	June 2	Caripito, Venezuela	750
Caripito, Venezuela	June 3	Paramaribo, Suriname (Dutch Guiana)	667
Paramaribo, Suriname	June 4	Fortaleza, Brazil	1200
Fortaleza, Brazil	June 6	Natal, Brazil	268
Natal, Brazil	June 7	St. Louis, Senegal (French West Africa)	1961
St. Louis, Senegal	June 8	Dakar, Senegal	103
Dakar, Senegal	June 10	Gao, Mail (French West Africa)	1130
Gao, Mali	June 11	Ndjamena, Chad (Fort Lamy, French Equatorial Africa)	989
Ndjamena, Chad	June 12	Al Fasher, Sudan (Anglo-Egyptian Sudan)	700
Al Fasher, Sudan	June 13	Khartoum, Sudan	501
Khartoum, Sudan	June 13	Massawa, Ethiopia (Italian Eritrea)	450
Massawa, Ethiopia	June 14	Assab, Ethiopia	300
Assab, Ethiopia	June 15	Karachi, Pakistan (India)	1600
Karachi, Pakistan	June 17	Calcutta, India	1390
Calcutta, India	June 18	Sittwe, Myanmar (Akyab, Burma)	335
Sittwe, Myanmar	June 19	Rangoon, Myanmar	306
Rangoon, Myanmar	June 20	Bangkok, Thailand (Siam)	300
Bangkok, Thailand	June 20	Singapore, Malaysia (British Crown Colony)	904
Singapore, Malaysia	June 21	Bandung, Java, Indonesia (Dutch East Indies)	560
Bandoeng, Java	June 24	Soerabaja, Java, Indonesia	355
Soerabaja, Java, Indonesia	June 25	Bandung, Java, Indonesia	355
Bandoeng, Java, Indonesia	June 27	Koepang, Timor, Indonesia	1165
Koepang, Timor, Indonesia	June 28	Port Darwin, Australia	500
Port Darwin, Australia	June 29	Lae, Papua New Guinea (Territory of New Guinea)	1207
Lae, Papau New Guinea	July 2	Howland Island, U.S. Territory	2556
Howland Island		Honolulu, Oahu, Hawaii (Territory of Hawaii)	1900
Honolulu, Hawaii		Oakland, California	2410

Total miles planned: 28, 595
Total miles flown (Oakland to vicinity of Howland Island): 24,285

think it was the *Ontario*. However, this ship's crew neither heard Earhart's message nor spotted her plane.

Meanwhile, T.H. Gude, a policeman on Nauru Island, had apparently been picking up Earhart's transmissions on a home radio set. He later reported that between 10:00 P.M. and 11:00 P.M., he heard her say that she was seeing Nauru's lights. Prior to her flight, Earhart had been told to watch for these huge floodlights, which were part of a mining operation; on a clear night, they would have been visible by air for well over one hundred miles. But again, the *Ontario* did not hear this transmission.

First Attempts to Reach the *Itasca*

By this time, the *Itasca* had begun sending weather reports and directional information to Earhart on the hour and the half hour, as requested, using both Morse code and voice transmission on frequencies of 7500, 3105, and 500. However, rather than use the time zone that Earhart had requested (GCT), they used local time, which meant that they were not broadcasting at times when Earhart would be listening.

Nonetheless, at 1415 GCT the *Itasca* finally heard Earhart's voice. She might have said something about the weather being overcast, but the *Itasca*'s chief radio operator, Leo G. Bellarts, was unsure. (At this point, Bellarts was the only one who could hear Earhart, because he was operating the radio with headphones; he would later switch to speakers that everyone in the radio room could hear.) The strength of Earhart's radio signal was extremely weak.

At 1515 GCT, her voice was heard again, still faint, this time apparently saying, "Earhart. Overcast. Will listen on 3105 kilocycle on hour and half hour."[25] However, Bellarts later said that despite what was noted in his radio log, he did not recall Earhart saying "overcast."

The *Itasca* responded on a radio frequency of 3105 kilocycles, saying: "What is your position? When do you expect to arrive Howland? Please acknowledge this message on your next schedule."[26] Instead of answering at the scheduled time—which the *Itasca* was still determining by local time—Earhart interrupted a weather report transmission at 1623 GCT, with a faint, static-ridden message. Her only intelligible words were "partly cloudy."[27]

"Will Whistle in Microphone"

At 1744 GCT, Earhart transmitted another message: "Want bearing on 3105 kilocycles on hour. Will whistle in microphone."[28] This time her radio signal was a little stronger, and it would continue to increase in strength with each subsequent message. Earhart was apparently coming closer to the *Itasca*'s location off Howland Island.

By this time, the ship's captain, Cdr. Warner K. Thompson, had sent some of his men to Howland Island with a direction finder capable of working on a frequency of 3105. Contributed by Earhart's representative on board the *Itasca*, Richard Black of the U.S. Department of the Interior, this high-frequency direction finder was far less reliable than the *Itasca*'s direction finder, though it would work at greater distances. However, at 1745 GCT, when Earhart repeated her request for a bearing, the men on Howland Island discovered that their high-frequency direction finder was not working; its battery was low.

At 1815 GCT, Earhart called out again: "Please take bearing on us and report in a half hour. I will make noise in microphone. About one hundred miles out."[29] The *Itasca* still could not take a bearing, but radio operators were unsure when to respond. Earhart had said she would be listening for their answer "in a half hour," but previously she had always used the phrase "on the half hour." Did she make a mistake this time?

After some discussion, the operators waited a half hour to respond: "Cannot take a bearing on 3105 very well. Please

send on 500 or do you wish to take a bearing on us?"[30] Five more times, *Itasca* radio operators repeated their request for Earhart to transmit on 500. However, with no trailing wire, Earhart could not send at 500 kilocycles. Even had she been able to send on 500, though, since this message was sent in Morse code, Earhart would not have understood it.

"Gas Is Running Low"

When not transmitting messages, the *Itasca* continued to listen for Earhart on 3105, 7500, and 500. At 1912 GCT (around 7:42 A.M.), the ship's radio operators again received a voice transmission from Earhart on 3105. She said, "We must be on you but cannot see you, but gas is running low. We have been unable to reach you by radio. We are flying at 1,000 feet."[31] According to some witnesses, she also said, "Only one-half hour gas left."[32]

A minute later, after the *Itasca* had answered this message, Earhart said, "Earhart calling *Itasca*. We are circling but cannot hear you. Go ahead on 7500 either now or on the schedule time on half hour."[33] Her voice was loud and clear, as though she was very close. The *Itasca* answered immediately on 7500—and this time, Earhart heard the message. At 2013 GCT (around 8:00 A.M.), again loud and clear, she said: "We received your signals but unable to get a [bearing]. Please take bearing on us and answer on 3105 with voice."[34] Earhart still did not apparently understand that although she could communicate with the *Itasca* on higher frequencies, they needed to take their bearings on lower frequencies.

At 8:44 A.M., Earhart made her last transmission to the *Itasca*, an enigmatic message regarding her position: "We are on the line of position 157 dash 337. Will repeat this message. We will repeat this message on 6210 KC. Wait listening on 6210 KC. We are running north and south."[35] Regarding this last phrase, the radio operator failed to note Earhart's exact words as she said them, so he had to add the words to his log later. Scribbled in a tight space, these words could also be "running on north and south line" or "running on line north and south." Some people have suggested that she might instead have said "running on line north to south."[36]

What Line of Position?

In any case, the *Itasca* radio operators were puzzled by the numbers in Earhart's message. The phrase "line of position" was open to interpretation. Could she have meant a line of longitude or a line of latitude? Part of a mapping grid imagined on the globe, latitude lines run from east to west and longitude lines run from north to south; their positions are identified by the direction and degree to which they are distant from, respectively, the equator or the prime meridian (an imaginary line running from North Pole to South Pole). Howland Island, for example, is located at 0.8 north latitude and 176.633 east longitude.

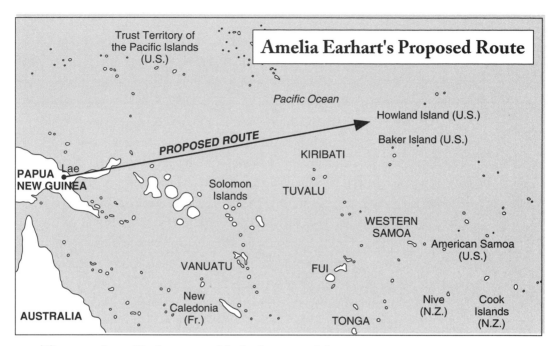

The numbers Earhart provided, then, could not represent points of latitude and longitude, given that she was flying somewhere near Howland. Instead they sounded like two references to longitude. Did this mean that Earhart was saying she was lost somewhere between the longitude lines of 156 degrees and 337 degrees? This north-south band represented such a large area that Earhart's information would not be very helpful.

Consequently Thompson (and, later, Mantz as well) decided that when Earhart said "line of position" she meant not a line of longitude but a sun line, which a navigator can determine based on a sextant observation of the sun. When drawn perpendicular to the direction of the rising sun, this line would have pointed toward 156 degrees on a compass one way, and 337 degrees the other way, cutting across Earhart's course to Howland at a slight slant, from southeast (337) to northwest (157). More important, by considering the time of sunrise, Noonan could have used this line to calculate how far east or west of Howland Island the Electra was, though not how far north or south. So if Earhart said she was "running north and south," she probably meant that Noonan was having her fly up and down, roughly north and south, trying to find where Howland was along a compass line of 156–337.

Given the vagueness of Earhart's comments, however, radio operators on the *Itasca* knew that the best way to locate the Electra was by taking a bearing. But to do this, they needed Earhart to hear and understand their instructions. In their next message, then, they asked her to stay on 3105. She did not respond to this transmission, or to any subsequent ones. Her last message to the *Itasca* was at 8:43 A.M. local time, when she had been in the air around nineteen hours.

However, a radio station on Nauru Island heard her voice three more times. Her messages were unintelligible, and the operator was unable to make contact with her. Nonetheless, Radio Nauru's operators immediately notified the Coast Guard of her messages, stating: "Speech not interpreted owing bad modulation or speaker shouting into microphone but voice similar to that emitted in flight last night with exception no hum of plane in background."[37] After this, the Nauru operators continued to listen for Earhart. Neither they nor the *Itasca* heard her voice again.

Chapter 4

A Crash or a Landing?

A short time after Earhart's last communication to the *Itasca*, at 8:47 A.M., Thompson called his men back from Howland Island and prepared to go looking for the Electra. He was not yet willing to officially declare her lost, but rather overdue for her destination. Still, he worried that this delay would cost Earhart her life. Was it possible that she was now floating on the ocean in a wrecked plane, hoping for rescue? Could she have managed to land on one of the many uninhabited small islands around Howland, alive but perhaps injured? Or was she already dead, having crashed her plane nose-first into the sea?

Searching the Sea

While continuing to send messages to Earhart on 500, 3105, and 7500 kilocycles, Thompson tried to figure out where she might be. Since her voice had been clear in her last transmissions, he decided that she must have been sending them from no more than one hundred miles away from his location near Howland Island. He also felt that she had been flying in heavy clouds north, west, or northwest of the island, because all of the other areas around the island were clear enough for him to have seen her plane.

Earhart demonstrates inflating her plane's life raft. Without the raft, which she may have left in New Guinea, surviving a crash in the open ocean would have been improbable.

By around 10:00 A.M., Thompson knew that the Electra could not possibly still be in the air, given its fuel load. However, he hoped that Earhart had been able to make a dead-stick landing on the ocean. This difficult maneuver would have required the pilot to glide without engine power, but if successful, the Electra would be afloat and Earhart and Noonan would be able to climb out of the plane before it sank. Still, their survival time on the open ocean would be limited, particularly if Harry Balfour was correct about Earhart leaving their life raft behind in Lae.

At 10:40 A.M., nearly two hours after he had last heard from Earhart, Thompson officially declared Earhart lost and notified his superiors of this fact. He then headed his ship toward the area northwest of Howland where he thought the

Electra would have gone down. Setting his course for 337 degrees, he planned to search along the 157–337 sun line, northwest of Howland. Later, however, naval officers in Honolulu would decide that Earhart was on this line to the southeast of Howland Island. They dispatched a U.S. battleship, the *Colorado*, to search this area.

Eventually other ships joined the search around Howland as well: the *Ontario*, the *Swan*, the aircraft carrier *Lexington*, three U.S. destroyers, a British freighter, and two Japanese navy ships. In all, sixty-five airplanes (sixty of them from the *Lexington*) and ten ships covered 250,000 square miles of open ocean. Their efforts to find any sign of Earhart or her plane lasted sixteen days, during which they were hampered by rough seas and intermittent rain.

The USS Lexington *searches for Earhart and her plane.*

Conflicting Stories

After Earhart's disappearance, comments made by her friends and relatives only fueled the controversy over the circumstances of her flight and her possible fate. In his book *Eyewitness: The Amelia Earhart Incident*, Thomas E. Devine reports:

In a 1949 interview, Earhart's mother, Amy Otis Earhart, claimed, "Amelia told me many things, but there were some things that she couldn't tell me. I am convinced she was on some sort of government mission, probably on verbal orders." Yet in 1962, Eleanor Roosevelt [widow of the late U.S. president Franklin D. Roosevelt] told Earhart's sister, Muriel Earhart Morrissey, "Franklin and I loved Amelia too much to send her to her death." Mrs. Morrissey says that "Amelia's plane went down near Howland Island because of a radio failure—the Coast Guard Cutter could not home her in." Ann Holtgren Pellegreno, who duplicated Earhart's 1937 flight in 1967, claims, "It is very difficult, if not impossible, to believe she just went down." Nancy Tier, a good friend of Earhart's and a fellow pilot, states with assurance, "I believe very confidently she was on Saipan [in Japanese custody]."

Earhart's mother (left) and sister gave conflicting stories about the circumstances of the doomed flight.

Mysterious Radio Signals

During this period, several people reported hearing faint or garbled radio transmissions that they believed to be from Earhart. Of these, the most credible were four independent reports from radio operators in Los Angeles, California. According to a message the U.S. government sent to the *Itasca* on July 4, these men "reported receiving Earhart's voice this morning . . . position given as . . . southwest Howland Island. . . . Heard on 3105 KCS and call [letters] of plane distinctly heard and verified. . . ."[38] Based on this message, the *Itasca* headed southwest of Howland Island and searched a two thousand square-mile area there.

At 3:25 P.M. Pacific Standard Time (PST) on July 5, government officials decided that Earhart's radio would no longer have the power to send messages. This meant that all further reports of hearing her voice could be considered mistakes or hoaxes. However, after consulting with experts on the Electra's design, the government also determined that if the plane had survived a dead-stick landing, it could still be floating on the surface of the water—probably, as one message to the *Itasca* and the *Colorado* stated, "on original line of position . . . through Howland Island and Phoenix Group. . . ."[39]

Island Searches

In mentioning the Phoenix Group, the government's message was referring to a group of uninhabited islands about 350 miles southeast of Howland. The *Colorado* was responsible for searching these islands, using three floatplanes that were launched from its deck via catapults. During this aerial search, no one saw any evidence of plane wreckage on the islands, though one of the pilots recorded that one, Gardner Island, showed "signs of recent habitation."[40] What these signs were, however, was not noted. Moreover, the captain of the *Colorado* decided not to put a shore party on the island, fearing that if he came close enough to Gardner to do so, his ship would run aground on a reef.

Meanwhile, another group of ships searched the Gilbert Islands, a group of islands west of Howland. The rationale for searching in this direction was that Earhart might have tried to turn back to Lae. However, these islands were populated, and no one living on them claimed to have seen Earhart.

On July 19 the U.S. government called off the search, declaring that the Electra must have crashed into the sea without leaving any wreckage behind. But George Putnam was not willing to accept this conclusion. Convinced that his wife was still adrift at sea, he offered a reward of two thousand dollars to anyone who could provide him with information about Earhart's location. As a result, he received numerous tips from psychics and spiritual mediums who claimed that Earhart was a castaway on a deserted island.

Determined to rescue his wife, Putnam sent two small ships to visit the Phoenix Islands, the Gilbert Islands, some reefs near the Gilbert Islands, and parts of the Marshall Islands, which were northwest of Howland Island. Due to rough seas and rocky shorelines, the ships' crewmen did not go ashore on all of these islands, but they did manage to get close enough to study their beaches for signs of a castaway or plane wreckage. They found neither.

A Spy Mission

After clinging to hope for many months, Putnam finally accepted the fact that Earhart was no longer alive, and he petitioned government officials to officially declare her dead. They did so on January 5, 1939, less than two years after her disappearance. For many years, however, even after he remarried, Putnam occasionally looked into rumors regarding Earhart's fate.

One of the most persistent rumors, beginning in the 1940s shortly after the Japanese attack on Pearl Harbor, was that Earhart was a prisoner of the Japanese. At the time of

Earhart's flight, Japan had been aggressively expanding its influence in the Pacific, and the U.S. military feared that the country was establishing a military installation on one of the Marshall Islands, in violation of a mandate from the international organization known as the League of Nations. Consequently, after Earhart disappeared, some people began to suspect that her attempt to circumnavigate the globe had been a cover for a spy mission. Earhart, they reasoned, had flown over the Pacific so that she could take photographs of the Marshall Islands.

Putnam insisted that Earhart had never worked as a spy. Moreover, when he investigated rumors that Earhart had been seen in Japanese custody, he found no evidence to support them.

George Putnam (sitting) uses maps to chart his wife's failed 1937 flight. It was many months before he accepted that she was dead.

Actress Rosalind Russell plays a character based on Amelia Earhart in Flight for Freedom, *a film that portrayed Earhart as a spy.*

He did, however, voice his suspicion that the U.S. government might have used its search for Earhart's downed plane as a chance to do some spying of its own. This accusation was also made in an October 16, 1937, issue of *Smith's Weekly*, an Australian newspaper.

A Japanese Captive

In 1943, RKO Pictures released a movie called *Flight For Freedom*, which was based on the notion that Earhart had been part of a Marshall Islands spy mission. This fueled rumors that the Japanese had imprisoned Earhart as a spy. Interest in the theory waxed and waned. As late as the early 1960s, a few people who had been in the Pacific during World War II claimed to have seen Earhart in Japanese custody.

The place most often mentioned in these reports was Saipan, in the Mariana Islands, with the first significant reference to this location appearing in Capt. Paul L. Briand Jr.'s 1960 book *Daughter of the Sky*. An English professor at the U.S. Air Force Academy, Briand theorized that Earhart's plane had crashed near Saipan, and that the Japanese had captured and executed both her and Noonan. Much of this theory was based on an account from a Saipan native, Josephine Blanco Akiyama, who was eleven years old when Earhart disappeared. Akiyama claimed that she had seen an American plane crash in a harbor, witnessed soldiers leading its two passengers—a man and a short-haired young woman—into nearby woods, and heard two shots ring out. She never saw the Americans again.

After reading Briand's book, Fred Goerner, a journalist in San Francisco, California, decided to check out Akiyama's

Journalist Fred Goerner loads aircraft wreckage onto a boat while researching stories that Earhart survived the plane crash.

story for himself. He went to Saipan four times, interviewed dozens of natives, and found a few who also claimed to have seen two American flyers taken captive by the Japanese. However, there was a crucial difference between most of these stories and Akiyama's: Earhart had not been executed, but was held prisoner for several months before dying of some illness.

One of the people Goerner interviewed, Matilde San Nicolas, said that she had seen a woman fitting Earhart's description in Japanese custody. Under guard, this woman was allowed to go on a daily walk. San Nicolas claimed to have given the woman fruit on one such occasion, and reported that Earhart later gave her a ring in return. This ring, however, had been lost, according to San Nicolas, who also said that shortly after this exchange the woman died of dysentery.

Another Goerner interviewee, a grocer named José Pangelinan, said that he had seen both Earhart and Noonan in captivity (though, like San Nicholas, Pangelinan had not known it was them at the time). Earhart, he said, was kept in an inn until she died of some disease, while Noonan was kept in a military stockade until the Japanese executed him. Pangelinan claimed that the two were buried together just outside an old cemetery.

Goerner searched for the grave and found one near this site, but subsequent analysis of the bones it contained revealed that none of the four people these bones belonged to were Caucasian. Goerner also found an airplane's generator in the harbor where Earhart's plane had supposedly crashed, but it was not from an American-made plane. Nonetheless, Goerner believed that there was some truth to the stories he had heard.

Crash on an Atoll

In 1966 Goerner published *The Search for Amelia Earhart*, in which he suggested that Earhart and Noonan had crash-landed on an atoll in the Marshall Islands and that they had indeed been part of a spying mission over the nearby Caroline Islands.

The pair was later rescued by a Japanese fishing boat, Goerner said, which took the Americans to a Japanese naval ship, which in turn took them to Saipan. Goerner further theorized that the airplane Akiyama claimed to have seen in the harbor was not Earhart's, but a Japanese military plane transferring her and Noonan from ship to shore. Goerner accused the U.S. government of hiding information about Earhart's capture to cover up her spying mission.

Was Earhart in the United States?

In the late 1960s and early 1970s, other writers theorized that Earhart had not only been a Japanese captive, but that she had survived the war and eventually returned to the United States. One such book, *Amelia Earhart Lives* by Joe Klass and Joseph Gervais, reported that after the war, the Japanese had set Earhart free, whereupon she returned to the United States disguised as a Roman Catholic nun to preserve her anonymity. By 1970, Klass and Gervais said, Earhart was living in New Jersey under a pseudonym, happy to have left the stress of her past life of fame behind. They contended that a woman named Irene Bolam was really Earhart.

Bolam denied being Earhart, though she admitted that she was a former aviator, had belonged to the same aviation organizations as Earhart, and had known Earhart personally. When *Amelia Earhart Lives* was published in 1970, she successfully sued to have it pulled from circulation. Even after this court battle, though, the authors continued to insist that Bolam was Earhart.

Government Conspiracy Accusations

During the 1980s several more books were published touting the Japanese captive theory. In 1985 *Amelia Earhart: The Final Story*, by former air force officer Victor Loomis, supported the idea that Earhart crashed on an atoll near the Marshall Islands. In fact, he claimed that he had stumbled upon her plane's wreckage on the Eniwetok Atoll, where he had been stationed during the 1950s. Others who looked for this wreckage were unable to find it, however. Loomis believed that Earhart had been imprisoned by the Japanese and died in captivity, but he was not convinced that she had been on a spying mission. Instead, he suspected that she had merely gotten lost en route to Howland Island.

Sharing this view was Thomas Devine, a U.S. Marine sergeant who had been stationed in the Pacific during and after World War II. But in his 1987 book *Eyewitness: The Amelia Earhart Incident,* he said that Earhart's guilt or innocence was immaterial, because the Japanese would have believed that any foreigner who had flown over one of their military bases was a spy. Devine said:

Irene Bolam, holding a copy of Amelia Earhart Lives, *denounces the book's contention that she is the doomed pilot.*

Many researchers refuse the spy mission theory, but in 1937 nothing would have dissuaded the Japanese from such a thought. They became increasingly suspicious when American radio broadcasts insisted that Earhart and Noonan were down near Howland Island, and when the Navy moved near forbidden waters to search for the missing flyers.[41]

Not only was Devine sure that the Japanese had imprisoned Earhart, but he believed that the U.S. government was concealing this information from the public. Specifically, he thought that right before the end of World War II, the government had found Earhart's plane, realized the Japanese had been responsible for her death, and decided to hide this information to protect America's postwar relationship with Japan. He explained why:

> In July 1944, the Secretary [U.S. Secretary of the Navy James Forrestal] was looking beyond the end of the Second World War. . . . He knew that a healthy world economy was vital . . . and believed it was essential for German and Japanese industry to be rebuilt and stimulated. . . . Containing communist expansion depended on Japanese recovery and Western cooperation, which would be jeopardized by disclosing Japanese mistreatment of an American heroine with the magnetism of Amelia Earhart.[42]

In support of his theory, Devine claimed to have seen officials from the U.S. military, including James Forrestal, destroying Earhart's plane with an explosive device at a military airfield in 1944. He said he knew it was the Electra because it had the same unique identification number, NR16020. He also suggested that Forrestal's death in 1947 was part of the government coverup. By this time Forrestal had been committed to a naval hospital because of mental illness; shortly thereafter he fell out of an upper-floor window. This death was ruled a suicide, but Devine contended that Forrestal had been murdered to keep him from revealing what he knew about Earhart.

According to one theory, U.S. Navy Secretary James Forrestal (pictured) and other government officials destroyed Earhart's plane in 1944.

"Running North to South"

In more recent years, arguments regarding whether or not Earhart was a Japanese captive have centered around her last radio transmission to the *Itasca*. After Earhart disappeared, most people accepted the government's claim that her last words were "running north and south." Now, though, it is clear that the *Itasca*'s radio log was unreliable on this point. And if Earhart had actually said "running north to south," then she would have been flying south toward Howland Island from the direction of the Marshall Islands.

If this was the case, then perhaps government officials, who received Earhart's flight plan prior to her trip, asked her to alter the Pacific leg of her journey in order to fly over and photograph Japanese naval bases in Jaluit in the Marshall Islands and Truk in the Eastern Caroline Islands. This detour would have only taken her a few hundred miles out of her way, and for the right price it might have seemed worth the risk. Moreover, Earhart might have considered it just as easy to find Howland from the north as from the west

Supporting this theory is the fact that one way to reach Howland from Jaluit is to turn southwest on a compass heading of 157, one of the numbers in Earhart's "line of position." And given the timing, this flight would have taken place before dawn, when it was too dark for the Japanese to see Earhart's plane. However, for Earhart to have made this detour, her radio reports to Harry Balfour, in which she indicated that she was on a direct course to Howland Island, had to have been lies.

Covering Up Incompetence

Some people who believe that Earhart approached Howland from the north also believe that the U.S. government intentionally changed her last words in order to hide her true location. But not all of these people think that the coverup was intended to hide a spy mission. Instead, they suggest that the government wanted to hide its incompetence. Under this theory, all of the vague reports about what Earhart said or did not say were part of an attempt to conceal the *Itasca*'s failures, and rumors that Noonan was a drunk and that Earhart did not understand her radio equipment were created to deflect blame from Thompson and onto the dead navigator and pilot.

Indeed, after Earhart disappeared, the navy commended Thompson for his search efforts, and many of his errors did not come to light until much later. Moreover, some evidence indicates that the government restricted access to certain key documents related to Earhart's disappearance; for example, when Paul Mantz asked to see the *Itasca*'s radio log in 1938, he apparently received an edited version that contained only nine of the original nineteen pages. Such reports of censorship led many people to believe that the government classified all Earhart-related documents in its possession. However, when a 1991 request for the mandatory declassification of all Earhart-related documents was granted under the Freedom of Information Act, no such classified documents were found.

Misstatements and Mistakes

It does seem, though, that Thompson misstated some of his actions on the day Earhart disappeared. For example, according to the ship's logs, the *Itasca* generated heavy black smoke that stretched for ten miles, an action that would have helped Earhart find the ship. But experts who have studied the *Itasca*'s method of smoke production, as well as wind conditions at the time, argue that the smoke could not have stretched so far and would have been neither heavy nor black. Similarly, although Thompson's radio and deck logs support his contention that Earhart used the word "overcast" when heavy clouds were northwest of Howland Island (which is why, he later said, he decided to search only in the northwest), studies of air pressure, wind conditions, and other factors suggest that cloud cover in the area was minimal and visibility was at least twenty miles.

Paul Mantz studies an aviation map. When he asked to see the Itasca's *radio log, Mantz received an edited version, fueling rumors of a government cover-up.*

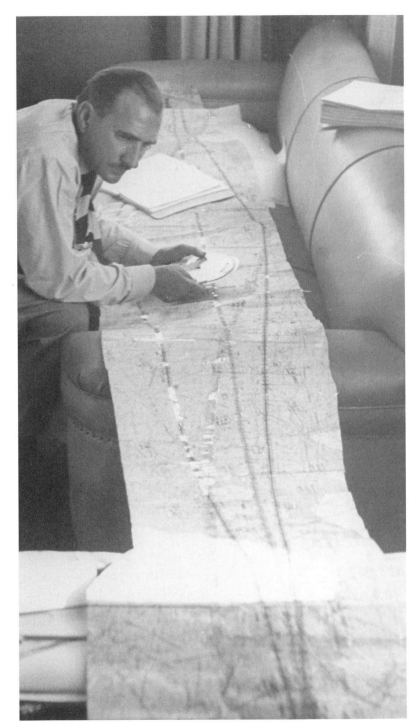

Even when considering apparently accurate *Itasca* records, it is clear that Thompson made numerous mistakes both during Earhart's flight and the subsequent search. While she was in the air, the *Itasca* should have been continuously rather than intermittently transmitting a beacon signal, to increase the chance that Earhart's direction finder could take a bearing on it. In addition, Thompson should have provided his men on Howland Island with a better battery for their direction finder; instead he gave them one with such inadequate storage capacity that it ran out of power long before it was really needed. The *Itasca*'s radio operators also made the mistake of transmitting at times when Earhart was scheduled to send them a message. Since the *Itasca*'s radio could not transmit and receive at the same time, this might have kept them from hearing her.

After Earhart disappeared, Thompson failed to conduct a thorough search along the 157–331 line of position. Since he believed that he knew how far away from Howland she was, he limited his search to a very specific area. He also assumed that he could see a plane floating on the water from as far as 5.6 miles away, which might not have been possible. In addition, Thompson conducted part of his search at night, during which he sometimes veered from his search pattern to check out lights he thought were signal flares. (They turned out to be shooting stars.) In one message to his superiors, he claimed to have searched fifteen hundred square miles during the night, though it was doubtful he could have scanned this much ocean with his searchlights.

Earhart's Skills

In researching Thompson's actions and purported errors, John P. Riley Jr., a radar officer who once served on the *Colorado*, found a transcript of a 1938 telephone conversation between a White House secretary and Secretary of the Treasury Henry Morgenthau Jr. In this conversation, Morgenthau speaks of not wanting to give Paul Mantz documents related to Earhart's disappearance because "it's just going to smear the whole reputation of Amelia Earhart."[43] Riley interpreted this to mean that Thompson had written reports and altered records to make Earhart look bad and himself look good. But others who have considered this telephone transcript suggest that if there was a government cover-up, then it was created only to protect the reputation of a national heroine.

Indeed, there is evidence to suggest that Earhart was far less competent than her public image—as constructed by Putnam—suggested. As her original navigator, Henry Manning, said, she tended to drift left as she flew, and over long distances this error could put her hundreds of miles off course. (And, in the case of her circumnavigation, it would have forced her to approach Howland Island from the north.) However, many aviation experts also note that although Earhart lived in a time when aviation accidents were common, she never had any major accidents prior to her disappearance; she was always able to walk away from a crash. Moreover, the errors on her fatal flight were primarily related to her lack of skill with a radio rather than with an airplane.

For this reason, some people, such as Elgen Long in his 1999 book *Amelia Earhart: The Mystery Solved*, say that Earhart was a good pilot who operated her Electra well, even though—at least according to Long—she not only lost her way but miscalculated her rate of fuel consumption. Long believes that this error resulted in Earhart crashing into the ocean, and he insists that she could not have survived this crash because her Electra had neither seatbelts nor shoulder harnesses. He has proposed that an expedition be launched that would use sonar equipment to search the bottom of the ocean near Howland

One researcher contends that Treasury Secretary Henry Morgenthau Jr. participated in a conversation about withholding documents related to Earhart.

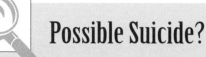

Possible Suicide?

Over the years since Earhart's disappearance, a few people have suggested that the aviator crashed her plane on purpose, deliberately killing herself. But Earhart biographer Jean L. Backus believes this scenario is the least likely of all:

> A rumor of suicide arises occasionally, and is only notable because it so entirely misrepresents the character of Amelia Earhart. It claims that being fed up with her marriage and tired of empty fame, or having an unsatisfactory affair with some man, or not wanting to retire into the obscurity of a research program at Purdue University or to face the physical deterioration of age, or perhaps already suffering a terminal illness, Amelia chose to "pop off" voluntarily. No one with the remotest understanding of and appreciation for her integrity as a human being, a woman, and a pilot could believe such a false and especially malicious rumor. To be sure, she dreaded retirement and old age, and as she said often, "When I go, I'd like best to go in my plane. Quickly." Still, it is a canard to suggest she would kill herself and willy-nilly take along another person.

Island. Long is certain that such an expedition would locate Earhart's plane and perhaps her body as well. Others, however, say that while Earhart's plane might have ended up in the sea, Earhart and Noonan made their way to shore, and that her remains are on a deserted island somewhere. The search for Amelia Earhart, then, continues.

Chapter 5

The Earhart Project

In the past few years, most of the attention related to Amelia Earhart's disappearance has been focused on efforts to find an island where she might have been stranded. These efforts began in 1998, when an organization called the International Group for Historic Aircraft Recovery (TIGHAR) turned its attention to trying to find Earhart's Pacific landing site. To this end, the group created the Earhart Project, dedicated to finding solid evidence to support the theory that Earhart died on a deserted island while awaiting rescue.

Adopting a New Idea

TIGHAR was originally certain that Earhart's plane had gone down in the open ocean. The group's original intent, then, was to find the location of the wreckage under the sea. To this end, TIGHAR's researchers examined a variety of Earhart-related documents, and eventually they decided that Earhart did not crash into the sea after all.

What convinced TIGHAR of this fact was their conclusion that—based on flight conditions, flight duration, and the Electra's rate of fuel consumption—Earhart would have had three to four hours of fuel left when she lost radio contact with the *Itasca*. They decided that at this time, Earhart had to have been south of Howland Island, flying along the 156–337 line of position. They further concluded that the direction of this flight had to be south—because, as TIGHAR board member Thomas King explains in his book *Amelia Earhart's Shoes:*

> A navigator who doesn't know whether he or she is north or south of the island and who directs the pilot to fly north has only a fifty-fifty chance of finding something—Howland—before running out of fuel and falling into the ocean. This, of course, is because there is nothing north of Howland for many, many miles. Turning south gives the navigator a much better chance of coming up on an island (although it may not be visible). If it turns out that the navigator's starting point is north of Howland, flying south will bring him or her upon Howland and Baker [islands]. If the starting point is south of Howland and Baker, the navigator will come upon Nikumaroro—which, incidentally, is a lot bigger than Howland or Baker

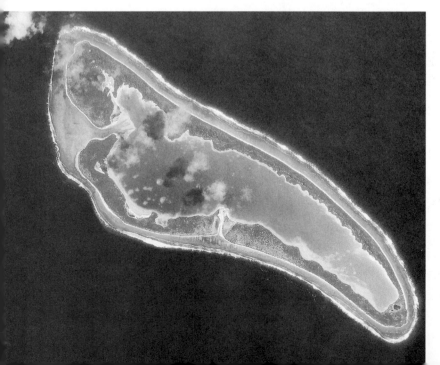

After retracing Earhart's flight path, TIGHAR concluded that she reached this small piece of land called Nikumaroro Island.

83

and, with its bright lagoon and tall trees, a good deal more visible from the air.[44]

At the time Earhart disappeared, Paul Mantz was also certain that she was flying southeastward on her line of position. By following this route, TIGHAR decided that Earhart and Noonan not only reached Nikumaroro Island—then called Gardner Island—but had enough fuel left to land on it. TIGHAR estimates that the pair would have been over this island, which is part of the Phoenix Islands, at 2400 GCT, or noon local time. At that hour, it would have been nearly low tide, when a relatively flat coral reef would have been close to the surface of the water. The reef would have looked like a good landing site; TIGHAR's official position is that Earhart had the skills to put her plane down at this spot.

"Love to Mother"

On August 21, 1945, someone sent a radiogram message from a Japanese prisoner-of-war camp, the Weihsein Internment Camp in China, to George Putnam via the U.S. State Department. This unsigned message read: "Camp liberated; all well. Volumes to tell. Love to mother." When this transmission was uncovered in the 1970s, many people believed that it had come from Earhart and proved she had survived the war as a Japanese captive. But in 2001, after a thorough investigation, the International Group for Historic Aircraft Recovery (TIGHAR) located a far more likely author of the message: Ahmad Kamal, a pilot, book author, and friend of Putnam's who had been imprisoned at Weihsein in 1942. TIGHAR reports:

According to [Kamal's] son, shortly after the camp was liberated, Kamal sent out two ra-

dio messages: one to Scribner and Sons about publishing a book, and one to George Putnam. His son said he has seen either notes or a journal of that message and could repeat it almost by heart—something like "camp liberated, all was well, volumes to follow and love to mother." The "love to mother" was added, said Kamal's son, because Putnam had agreed to look after Kamal's aging mother when Kamal left for China. Mrs. Kamal lived nearby and Putnam was to look in on her. . . . Kamal said his father often discussed Amelia Earhart and various disappearance theories. His father, who knew Amelia, said she was not at Weihsein while he was there from 1942 until August 1945.

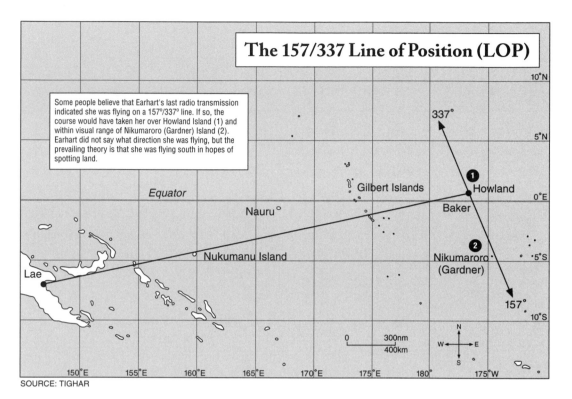

The 157/337 Line of Position (LOP)

Some people believe that Earhart's last radio transmission indicated she was flying on a 157°/337° line. If so, the course would have taken her over Howland Island (1) and within visual range of Nikumaroro (Gardner) Island (2). Earhart did not say what direction she was flying, but the prevailing theory is that she was flying south in hopes of spotting land.

SOURCE: TIGHAR

Looking for Wreckage

During the late 1990s and early 2000s, TIGHAR researchers repeatedly visited Nikumaroro, looking for the remains of Earhart and her plane. They also studied the history of the island, to see whether there had been any reports from people who had seen such remains. And, finally, they reviewed records from 1937 and 1938 to find out whether the island had been adequately searched at the time of Earhart's disappearance.

By studying historical records, TIGHAR learned that in 1937, government officials believed that Gardner Island and McKean Island, also in the Phoenix Islands, were the most likely land masses that Earhart would reach if she were flying along the line of position she had reported. This was one reason the USS *Colorado* was sent to investigate the area shortly after Earhart disappeared. At that time, the ship's captain, Wilhelm Friedell, reported that the pilots of his three floatplanes had seen no airplane wreckage, nor had they spotted Earhart or Noonan.

But TIGHAR believes that the wreckage and fliers might still have been there, even though they were not seen. Eight years earlier, in 1929, the SS *Norwich City* ran onto a reef at Gardner Island during a storm; while taking on water, the steamship caught fire. Those crew members that survived the incident were marooned on the island for several days, during which they salvaged some provisions from the wreck and established a campsite. According to TIGHAR, this story was well known among sailors, so when one of the *Colorado* pilots noticed signs of recent habitation on the island, he could well have assumed he was viewing the old campsite—particularly since no one appeared on the ground to signal for help as he circled overhead. In addition, the pilot might have thought that any metal debris—especially if it was scattered along the beach—were from the wreckage of the *Norwich City* rather than an airplane.

Tide levels at the time of the search also might have obscured the wreckage. A photograph taken from one of the *Colorado*'s planes on July 9, 1937, shows high tide and heavy surf on the reef where TIGHAR believes that the Electra landed. Rising water might have hidden airplane parts or washed them off the reef and into deep water, while the white sea spray of the surf might have obscured any remaining metal pieces.

Gardner Expeditions

Other observers are unconvinced by these arguments. TIGHAR's critics argue that even given these circumstances, the *Colorado*'s pilots would have noticed the larger pieces of an airplane wreckage. These critics also point out that in October 1937, just three months after Earhart disappeared, a British expedition exploring the island to determine whether it was suitable for settlement found no evidence of any wreckage. Neither did a New Zealand survey party during a two-month stay on the island from December 1938 to January 1939.

TIGHAR counters that neither group was looking for signs of Earhart, and they probably did not know that Gardner Island had once been considered a possible landing site for her plane. Moreover, both groups landed on the island on the south side of the *Norwich City* shipwreck, which would have masked any Electra wreckage from view. The New Zealanders had an added visibility problem; their visit to Gardner Island took place when heavy seas were pounding the reef. TIGHAR also points out that "on the southeastern side of the island in the same area . . . [the expedition] did come across 'signs of previous habitation' described as looking as if 'someone had bivouacked for the night.'"[45]

Estimating the Age of Bones

TIGHAR asked Karen Burns, a forensic osteologist (an expert on skeletal remains) to study Gerald B. Gallagher's notes regarding the bones found on Nikumaroro Island three years after Earhart's disappearance. According to Gallagher, these bones (now lost) looked at least four years old and therefore could not have been Earhart's. Burns explains her belief, however, that the bones were not nearly that old:

[Gallagher had] no experience on which to base his estimate. . . . How many people have experience with dead bodies lying in open tropical environments? Most people don't stick around to watch anything decompose. . . . [The Nikumaroro skeleton looked older] because it was on the surface of the ground on an equatorial island. . . . The conditions are less stable than they are underground. Things are always changing— day and night; storm and sun. And there's a greater array of diners. One hundred-plus pounds of food is a real treat—bring on the molds, algae, mosses, insects, birds, crabs, and rats. They find the body quicker, and . . . the work [of decomposition] is done efficiently and in short order. . . . When I think about hot places, I think about cases I've worked in Haiti or Georgia. Bodies in Georgia don't deteriorate quite as quickly as in Haiti, but skeletonization can take place in two weeks in the summertime. . . . In Haiti, I've worked with bones that were exposed for no more than a year, but most of the organic material was leached out. The bones were chalky white, cracked, and beginning to crumble.

Mysterious Bones

These signs of habitation were near a site where TIGHAR suspects that a skeleton once lay. This belief stems from TIGHAR's interview of Emily Sikuli, who had lived on Gardner Island as a child, from 1940 to 1941. Sikuli told TIGHAR that she had seen an airplane's wreckage "nearby that wrecked ship . . . on the rocky part . . . not far from where the waves break."[46] This would have been near the edge of the reef. Sikuli also said that the debris had been there for a while—and given that World War II had not yet broken out at that time, TIGHAR could be certain that the wreckage could not have been from a warplane.

When asked to further describe the wreckage, Sikuli said that her father would not let her go near it—but she had heard that bones were found there. She explained:

> Some [men] went to fish, they saw in the shallows some pools, at the place where the plane crashed, some bones, and they knew these were human bones because of the skull bone. . . . So it was arranged for a box to be made for the bones. . . . There were not many bones. . . . They do a search around that area but they found no other bones. Only these big bones that they found. I do not know how many. My father knew.[47]

Sikuli's father was a carpenter, and she claimed that he had built a box for the bones, which were then shipped off to Fiji.

A Trail of Telegrams

Following up on this story, TIGHAR verified that Sikuli had been one of fifty-eight colonists on Gardner Island, brought there as part of a British effort to relieve overcrowding and food shortages on other Pacific islands. The first such colonists arrived on the island in December 1938, less than eighteen months after Earhart's plane was lost. But again, these people did not know that Earhart might have landed on their island; their intent was to establish a village, not look for a plane wreck.

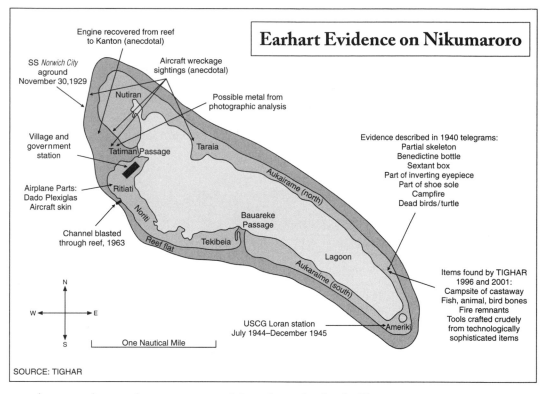

Earhart Evidence on Nikumaroro

Engine recovered from reef to Kanton (anecdotal)

SS *Norwich City* aground November 30, 1929

Aircraft wreckage sightings (anecdotal)

Nutiran

Possible metal from photographic analysis

Village and government station

Tatiman Passage

Taraia

Aukairame (north)

Evidence described in 1940 telegrams:
Partial skeleton
Benedictine bottle
Sextant box
Part of inverting eyepiece
Part of shoe sole
Campfire
Dead birds/turtle

Airplane Parts: Dado Plexiglas Aircraft skin

Ritiati

Noriti

Bauareke Passage

Channel blasted through reef, 1963

Reef flat

Tekibeia

Lagoon

Aukairame (south)

N
W — E
S

One Nautical Mile

USCG Loran station July 1944–December 1945

Ameriki

Items found by TIGHAR 1996 and 2001:
Campsite of castaway
Fish, animal, bird bones
Fire remnants
Tools crafted crudely from technologically sophisticated items

SOURCE: TIGHAR

Among those who were supervising the colonists' efforts was Gerald B. Gallagher, a British officer. TIGHAR discovered telegrams that Gallagher had exchanged with other government officials about the bones. One such telegram read:

> Some months ago a working party on Gardner discovered human skull—this was buried and I only recently heard about it. Thorough search has now produced more bones (including lower jaw) part of a shoe, a bottle and a sextant box. It would appear that
>
> (a) Skeleton is possibly that of a woman,
> (b) Shoe was a woman's and probably size 10,
> (c) Sextant box has two numbers on it 3500 (stenciled) and 1542—sextant being old fashioned and probably painted over with black enamel.

Bones look more than four years old to me, but there seems to be very slight chance that this may be remains of Amelia Earhardt. If United States authorities find that above evidence fits into general description, perhaps they could supply some dental information as many teeth are intact. Am holding latest finds for present but have not exhumed skull.

There is no indication that this discovery is related to wreck of the "Norwich City."[48]

In another telegram, Gallagher provided more details about the scene where the bones had been found:

British officer Gerald Gallagher (pictured) corresponded with British officials about human bones found on Nikumaroro Island that may have belonged to Earhart.

Bones were found on South East corner of island about 100 feet above ordinary high water springs. Body had obviously been lying under a "ren" tree and remains of fire, turtle, and dead birds appear to indicate life. All small bones have been removed by giant coconut crabs

which have also damaged larger ones. Difficult to estimate age of bones owing to activities of crabs but am quite certain they are not less than four years old and probably much older.

Only experienced man could state sex from available bones; my conclusion based on sole of shoe which is almost certainly a woman's.[49]

Clearly, then, the bones that Gallagher discovered were not located at the site described by Sikuli. Critics of TIGHAR's theories think this proves that Sikuli was an unreliable witness. However, TIGHAR suggests that there could have been two sites where bones were found; one set of remains might have belonged to Noonan and the other to Earhart. TIGHAR theorizes that one of them died at the crash site, while the other died elsewhere while searching for food and water.

Evaluating the Evidence

Gallagher shipped the bones to British officials in Suva, Fiji, in a box just like the one described by Sikuli. He also sent them the sextant box. TIGHAR found an acknowledgement that these items were received by British officials, but they have since disappeared, and TIGHAR has so far been unable to track them down.

In 1997, however, TIGHAR found sixteen British documents related to the discovery of these items. From these, the group knows that the British thought the bones were from some castaway, perhaps a Polynesian, who had died on the island at least twenty years before Gallagher found his skeleton. However, TIGHAR does not believe that such a conclusion could have been made with certainty. In fact, when TIGHAR provided a description of the bones, including detailed measurements noted in the British documents, to experts on bone analysis, these experts determined that the remains most likely belonged to a white woman of northern European descent who was approximately 5 feet 7 inches tall. This description would fit Amelia Earhart.

TIGHAR also discovered one document in which it is noted that the sextant box had a hand-stenciled identification number of 3500. The TIGHAR researchers examined another sextant box known to have been Noonan's and found that it had the number 3547 handwritten on the bottom. TIGHAR felt that the closeness of these two numbers was significant, particularly since Noonan once taught navigation. Thomas King, in *Amelia Earhart's Shoes*, says:

> So did Noonan have a collection of sextants, perhaps acquired during his career at sea, that he loaned to students, like a college professor loans books? Did he keep track of them with some kind of catalog system that featured numbers written —or stenciled—on their boxes? There's no way of knowing—as yet. But three things are sure: out of some 500 boxes examined by TIGHAR, only one had numbers on it; one of those numbers was similar to one of the numbers on the Niku [Gardner Island] box, and the box with that number once belonged to Fred Noonan.[50]

Continuing Research

TIGHAR has also investigated the possibility that the shoe Gallagher found might have been Earhart's. This shoe was a relatively narrow size 9 blucher oxford with a certain type of replacement heel, and Earhart

This photo of Nikumaroro Island was taken from a Navy search plane on July 9, 1937.

might have worn this type of shoe. But the possibility exists that someone on the island also wore such a shoe. From a 1940 inventory of the Gardner Cooperative Store, which had been set up for the colonists, TIGHAR learned that shoes were indeed available on Gardner Island. However, these shoes came from Australia and were unlikely to have been American-style oxfords. Still, TIGHAR acknowledges that the oxford could have come from many sources. King says:

> Members of the Woman's Army Corps (WACs) during World War II wore blucher-style oxfords, so it's conceivable that a WAC found her way to Nikumaroro and lost a shoe. . . . [And] it's conceivable that an unreported woman . . . [on a survey team] lost a shoe. . . . It's possible that someone came by in a yacht. But then, it's possible that the shoe was washed up in a storm wave, dropped from an airplane, or coughed up by a whale; there's really no end to the possibilities. None of the alternatives identified so far are very persuasive, but research continues.[51]

TIGHAR's Earhart Project also continues to look for airplane wreckage on Nikumaroro, not only near the reef but elsewhere, and whenever its researchers find a piece of metal they try to determine whether it might have come from the Electra. So far they have identified a few pieces as possibly coming from an Electra, but these results are far from conclusive. In fact, one of the main critics of TIGHAR's work, Elgen Long, insists that none of these pieces could have come from Earhart's plane. Long, a retired airline pilot, remains convinced that the Electra is somewhere at the bottom of the ocean, and believes that if it had ever been on Nikumaroro, TIGHAR would have found evidence of it by now.

TIGHAR disagrees. In fact, the Earhart Project has said that given its hypotheses regarding where the plane landed, there would be little left of the craft by now. The group presents this scenario as being most likely:

The airplane on the reef is destroyed by surf action and the debris is scattered "downstream" across the reef-flat, along the shoreline, and into the lagoon. During the island's period of habitation (1938–1963) the colonists encounter, and in some cases recover and use, various bits of wreckage. Those components recovered by the colonists are mostly consumed in local uses such as fishing tackle and decorative items. . . . Some wreckage may rest in deep water offshore.[52]

It is equally unclear what became of the store of provisions left on the island by the *Norwich City* survivors. One of these survivors, Daniel Hamer, reported, "Before leaving camp all provisions etc., were placed in the shelter, but I sincerely hope that no one will ever be so unfortunate as to need them."[53] However, a 1938 photograph of their camp, taken by the surveying New Zealanders, shows the provisions scattered in disarray. Could Earhart have disturbed this camp in a search for food and medical supplies?

A Teenager's Notebook

TIGHAR believes that this scenario is likely. Having examined radio transmissions made after Earhart lost contact with the *Itasca*, the group has decided that several messages could have come from Earhart. During transmissions, no airplane sounds were audible in the background, suggesting that the craft had landed. Moreover, none was transmitted after July 5, when Earhart's radio would have run out of power. These messages cannot be taken as conclusive evidence, though, since they were too garbled to understand.

Other indirect, but tantalizing, evidence exists that Earhart survived long enough to send some radio messages. TIGHAR uncovered the notebook of a woman named Betty, who was a teenager living in Florida when Earhart disappeared. In July 1937 she used this notebook, which functioned as her diary, to record a transmission she heard over her parents' shortwave radio. The message was from a woman calling for help, a man's voice in the background. At times the two seemed to be arguing, though the man's part of the conversation was faint and muddled. Some of the words that Betty wrote down were "Waters knee deep—let me out," "George," and "Watch that battery."[54]

Similar radio calls had been reported by people in Texas, Vermont, and Canada, but Betty's was the only one involving a written record made at the time the call for help supposedly took place. King reports, "Analysis of the notebook is ongoing, but so far it looks authentic. The right kind of notebook for the period, and all the songs and movies noted in it were popular around the time of Earhart's disappearance. . . . Betty herself, . . . interviewed in November 2000, seems to be a very credible witness."[55] In addition, radio experts have told TIGHAR that it is possible for someone living in Florida to have heard a transmission from the South Pacific, given certain weather conditions and frequencies.

Earhart's Last Hours

TIGHAR theorizes, then, that Earhart and Noonan both survived a landing on Nikumaroro, though the Electra was badly damaged. Eventually they left the wreckage, and one or both went to look for food. Consequently they might have been deep in the brush when the *Colorado*'s planes flew over, and were unable to get out into the open in time to signal their potential rescuers. In fact, even if they were still on the beach they might have been missed, because, as King says, from the air "little things like people are hard to see in the complicated visual environment of a tropical island."[56]

After this, the pair would not have survived on Nikumaroro for long. Water was scarce, and finding enough food would have taken more energy than either likely had left after such a long and demanding flight. In addition, any injuries they might have suffered during the landing would probably have become infected.

A front-page news story from 1937 kept alive rumors that Earhart had survived the plane crash.

Though the Earhart Project has not uncovered any hard evidence that Earhart and Noonan died on Nikumaroro (an idea TIGHAR calls the Nikumaroro Hypothesis), TIGHAR plans to continue its investigation of this theory. The group is still trying to locate the exact site where Gallagher found the bones he sent to Fiji, and to learn what happened to those bones. TIGHAR will also continue to visit Nikumaroro, looking for and carefully studying any bones, pieces of metal, or other artifacts it finds, and eventually it would like to search the deep waters around the island for signs of Earhart's Electra.

The group is confident that its Nikumaroro Hypothesis is correct. In addition, TIGHAR members suggest that the other two prevailing Earhart theories—that she either crashed in the open ocean or was captured by the Japanese—would be impossible to prove. About the latter, King says that people claiming to have seen Earhart on Saipan were unreliable witnesses, and "the chances of finding reliable evidence on Saipan is virtually nil—assuming it was ever there in the first place."[57] About the former, King says that TIGHAR does not have the financial resources to search the bottom of the ocean for the Electra's wreckage, adding that "anyone who thinks he can pinpoint where the plane crashed and sank, we think, is fooling himself."[58]

But David Jourdan, the founder of a maritime exploration company called Nauticos, disagrees with this opinion. In March 2002, in association with TIGHAR critic Elgen Long, Jourdan launched a $1.7 million Nauticos expedition to search for Earhart's plane on the ocean floor within one hundred miles west of Howland Island. Using sophisticated sonar equipment at a depth of eighteen thousand feet, Nauticos intended to cover an area of approximately six hundred square nautical miles, but after six weeks its equipment failed, and the company had to give up without finishing the search. Jourdan is currently deciding whether to resume his efforts, and other ocean explorers are trying to raise funds for similar expeditions.

These explorers believe it unlikely that Earhart found a landing site before her fuel ran out. It is equally unlikely, they say, that Earhart would have been able to land her plane successfully on a reef—particularly given her fatigue, health problems, and previous trouble with landings. "She couldn't see the island," insists Jourdan. "We believe she went into the water and her plane sank."[59]

But unless Nauticos or some other deep-sea expedition finds Earhart's plane at the bottom of the sea—or TIGHAR finds evidence of her presence on an uninhabited island—Amelia Earhart's fate will remain a mystery.

Notes

Introduction: A Mysterious Disappearance

1. Anne Morrow Lindbergh, *Hour of Gold, Hour of Lead: Diaries and Letters of Anne Morrow Lindbergh, 1929–1932.* New York: Harcourt Brace Jovanovich, 1973, p. 216.
2. Amelia Earhart, *Last Flight*, arranged by George Palmer Putnam. New York: Harcourt Brace, 1937, p. 55.

Chapter 1: Who Was Amelia Earhart?

3. Quoted in Donald M. Goldstein and Katherine V. Dillon, *Amelia: The Centennial Biography of an Aviation Pioneer.* Washington, DC: Brassey's, 1997, p. 21.
4. Quoted in Doris L. Rich, *Amelia Earhart: A Biography.* Washington, DC: Smithsonian Institution, 1989, p. 33.
5. Amelia Earhart, *The Fun of It: Random Records of My Own Flying and of Women in Aviation.* New York: Brewer, Warren & Putnam, 1932, p. 28.
6. Earhart, *The Fun of It*, p. 84.
7. Muriel Earhart Morrissey, *Courage Is the Price: The Biography of Amelia Earhart.* Wichita, KS: McCormick Armstrong, 1963, pp. 187–88.
8. Quoted in Rich, *Amelia Earhart,* p. 155.
9. Quoted in Rich, *Amelia Earhart,* p. 196.

Chapter 2: A Plan to Circle the Globe

10. Quoted in Thomas E. Devine with Richard M. Daley, *Eyewitness: The Amelia Earhart Incident.* Frederick, CO: Renaissance House, 1987, p. 9.
11. Quoted in Vincent V. Loomis with Jeffrey L. Ethell, *Amelia Earhart: The Final Story.* New York: Random House, 1985, pp. 47–48.
12. Loomis, *Amelia Earhart,* p. 49.
13. Quoted in Devine, *Eyewitness,* p. 11.
14. Loomis, *Amelia Earhart,* pp. 49–50.
15. Rich, *Amelia Earhart,* pp. 244–45.
16. Quoted in Loomis, *Amelia Earhart,* p. 56.
17. Quoted in Goldstein and Dillon, *Amelia,* p. 179.
18. Earhart, *Last Flight,* p. 79.

Chapter 3: A Doomed Flight

19. Don Dwiggins, *Hollywood Pilot: The Biography of Paul Mantz.* Garden

City, NY: Doubleday, 1967, p. 105.

20. Quoted in Loomis, *Amelia Earhart*, p. 61.

21. Thomas F. King, Randall S. Jacobson, Karen R. Burns, and Kenton Spading, *Amelia Earhart's Shoes: Is the Mystery Solved?* Walnut Creek, CA: AltaMira Press, 2001, p. 293.

22. King et al., *Amelia Earhart's Shoes*, pp. 292–93.

23. Quoted in Elgen M. Long and Marie K. Long, *Amelia Earhart: The Mystery Solved*. New York: Simon & Schuster, 1999, p. 177.

24. Quoted in Goldstein and Dillon, *Amelia*, p. 230.

25. Quoted in Rich, *Amelia Earhart*, p. 268.

26. Quoted in Rich, *Amelia Earhart*, p. 268.

27. Quoted in Long and Long, *Amelia Earhart: The Mystery Solved*, p. 208.

28. Quoted in Rich, *Amelia Earhart*, p. 269.

29. Quoted in Rich, *Amelia Earhart*, p. 269.

30. Quoted in King et al., *Amelia Earhart's Shoes*, p. 300.

31. Quoted in King et al., *Amelia Earhart's Shoes*, p. 300.

32. Quoted in Rich, *Amelia Earhart*, p. 269.

33. Quoted in Rich, *Amelia Earhart*, p. 269.

34. Quoted in Rich, *Amelia Earhart*, p. 269.

35. Quoted in Thomas E. Devine with Richard M. Daley, *Eyewitness: The Amelia Earhart Incident*, p. 20.

36. Note from Ric Gillespie, The Earhart Project Forum, TIGHAR, December 13, 1999, www.tighar. org/forum/highlights61_80/high lights66.html

37. Quoted in Goldstein and Dillon, *Amelia*, p. 235.

Chapter 4: A Crash or a Landing?

38. Quoted in Long and Long, *Amelia Earhart*, pp. 219–20.

39. Quoted in Long and Long, *Amelia Earhart*, p. 223.

40. "The Search for Amelia Earhart: An Overview," The Earhart Project, TIGHAR, www.tighar.org/Projects/ Earhart/AEoverview.html.

41. Devine, *Eyewitness*, p. 175.

42. Devine, *Eyewitness*, pp. 50–51.

43. John P. Riley Jr., "The Earhart Tragedy: Old Mystery, New Hypothesis," *Naval History*, August 2000, www. usni.org/ NavalHistory/Articles00/nhriley.htm.

Chapter 5: The Earhart Project

44. King et al., *Amelia Earhart's Shoes*, pp. 306–307.

45. "The British Exploratory Expedition," FAQs, TIGHAR, www.tighar. org/forum/FAQs/british.htm.

46. King et al., *Amelia Earhart's Shoes,* p. 276.

47. King et al., *Amelia Earhart's Shoes,* p. 277.

48. Quoted in King et al., *Amelia Earhart's Shoes,* p. 208.

49. Quoted in King et al., *Amelia Earhart's Shoes,* pp. 211–12.

50. King et al., *Amelia Earhart's Shoes,* p. 234.

51. King et al., *Amelia Earhart's Shoes,* p. 252.

52. "Hypothesis," The Earhart Project, TIGHAR, www.tighar.org/Projects/ Earhart/AEhypothesis. html.

53. Quoted in King et al., *Amelia Earhart's Shoes,* p. 254.

54. Quoted in King et al., *Amelia Earhart's Shoes,* p. 318.

55. King et al., *Amelia Earhart's Shoes,* p. 318.

56. King et al., *Amelia Earhart's Shoes,* p. 308.

57. King et al., *Amelia Earhart's Shoes,* p. 328.

58. King et al., *Amelia Earhart's Shoes,* p. 328.

59. Joanne Cavanaugh Simpson, "Looking for Amelia." *Johns Hopkins,* June 2002, www.jhu.edu/~jhumag/0602 web/amelia.html.

For Further Reading

Books

Jean L. Backus, ed., *Letters from Amelia, 1901–1937*. Boston: Beacon Press, 1982. This book is a compilation of Earhart's correspondence with various people.

Rober E. Bilstein, *Flight in America: 1900–1983*. Baltimore: Johns Hopkins University Press, 1984. This book provides an overview of the history of American aviation.

John Burke, *Winged Legend: The Story of Amelia Earhart*. New York: Putnam, 1970. This biography of the famous aviator includes illustrations.

Zachary Kent, *Charles Lindbergh and the* Spirit of St. Louis *in American History*. Berkeley Heights, NJ: Enslow, 2001. This book talks about Charles Lindbergh's historic flight across the Atlantic.

Eileen Morey, *Amelia Earhart*. San Diego, CA: Lucent Books, 1995. This book talks about Amelia Earhart's life and achievements.

Lynda Pflueger, *Amelia Earhart: Legend of Flight*. Berkeley Heights, NJ: Enslow, 2003. This easy-to-read biography offers basic information about Earhart's life.

Neta Snook Southern, *I Taught Amelia Earhart to Fly*. New York: Vantage, 1974. This autobiography was written by the woman pilot who was Earhart's first flying instructor.

Corinne Szabo, *Sky Pioneer: A Photobiography of Amelia Earhart*. Washington, DC: National Geographic Society, 1997. This book offers many excellent photographs related to Amelia Earhart's life.

Web Sites

Amelia Earhart Birthplace Museum (www.ameliaearhartmuseum.org). This site offers information about Amelia Earhart's life.

The International Group for Historic Aircraft Recovery (www.tighar.org). This site offers a huge volume of information about Amelia Earhart's final flight and the group's efforts to solve the mystery of her disappearance.

The Ninety-Nines: International Organization of Women Pilots (www.ninety-nines.org). The official Web site of the Ninety-Nines, an international organization of women pilots. Amelia Earhart was instrumental in founding the organization.

Works Consulted

Books

Jean L. Backus, *Letters from Amelia 1901–1937*. Boston: Beacon, 1982. This collection includes many of Earhart's letters to friends and family.

A Scott Berg, *Lindbergh*. New York: G.P. Putnam's Sons, 1998. This biography of Charles Lindbergh touches on the famous aviator's opinion of Amelia Earhart, who was frequently referred to as Lady Lindy.

Roger E. Bilstein, *Flight in America: 1900–1983*. Baltimore: Johns Hopkins University Press, 1984. This book offers a history of American aviation, from the Wright Brothers' first flight to the early flights of the space shuttle.

Susan Butler, *East to the Dawn: The Life of Amelia Earhart*. Reading, MA: Addison-Wesley, 1997. A thorough biography of the life of Amelia Earhart.

Thomas E. Devine with Richard M. Daley, *Eyewitness: The Amelia Earhart Incident*. Frederick, CO: Renaissance House, 1987. Thomas Devine, who claims to have witnessed the destruction of Earhart's plane on Saipan, offers his theories about the fate of Amelia Earhart and the U.S. government's attempts to cover it up.

Don Dwiggins, *Hollywood Pilot: The Biography of Paul Mantz*. Garden City, NY: Doubleday, 1967. A biography of the pilot and aviation expert who planned Amelia Earhart's famous flights.

Amelia Earhart, *The Fun of It: Random Records of My Own Flying and of Women in Aviation*. New York: Brewer, Warren & Putnam, 1932. Amelia Earhart's writings about some of her aviation experiences, as well as about the role of women in aviation.

———, *Last Flight*, arranged by George Palmer Putnam. New York: Harcourt Brace, 1937. Published posthumously, this is a collection of Amelia Earhart's writings about her around-the-world flight.

———, *20 Hrs., 40 Min.: Our Flight in the Friendship*. New York: G.P. Putnam's Sons, 1928. Amelia Earhart relates her experiences as a passenger on the airplane *Friendship* during its transatlantic flight.

Fred G. Goerner, *The Search for Amelia*

Earhart. Garden City, NY: Doubleday, 1966. Goerner discusses his theory that Amelia Earhart was captured by the Japanese and died in Saipan.

Donald M. Goldstein and Katherine V. Dillon, *Amelia: The Centennial Biography of an Aviation Pioneer.* Washington, DC: Brassey's, 1997. This book discusses Amelia Earhart's life and the circumstances surrounding her disappearance.

Thomas F. King, Randall S. Jacobson, Karen R. Burns, and Kenton Spading. *Amelia Earhart's Shoes: Is the Mystery Solved?* Walnut Creek, CA: AltaMira Press, 2001. This book explores TIGHAR's attempts to locate the uninhabited island where the group believes Earhart was stranded.

Anne Morrow Lindbergh, *Hour of Gold, Hour of Lead: Diaries and Letters of Anne Morrow Lindbergh, 1929–1932.* New York: Harcourt Brace Jovanovich, 1973. The wife of aviator Charles Lindbergh talks about many aspects of her life, including her impression of Amelia Earhart.

Elgen M. Long and Marie K. Long, *Amelia Earhart: The Mystery Solved.* New York: Simon & Schuster, 1999. Two of TIGHAR's main critics argue that Amelia Earhart had to have crashed in the open ocean and died on impact.

Vincent V. Loomis with Jeffrey L. Ethell, *Amelia Earhart: The Final Story.* New York: Random House, 1985. Loomis writes about his theory that Amelia Earhart died in Japanese captivity and his claims that he found the wreckage of her plane on an atoll in the Marshall Islands.

Mary S. Lovell, *The Sound of Wings: The Life of Amelia Earhart.* New York: St. Martin's Press, 1989. On its Web site, TIGHAR calls this book the best of the many biographies of Amelia Earhart.

Muriel Earhart Morrissey, *Courage Is the Price: The Biography of Amelia Earhart.* Wichita, KS: McCormick Armstrong, 1963. This biography of Amelia Earhart was written by her sister.

Doris L. Rich, *Amelia Earhart: A Biography.* Washington, DC: Smithsonian Institution, 1989. Part of the Smithsonian Institution's History of Aviation series, this biography primarily focuses on Amelia Earhart's life, but it also takes a position on her death: that she died after losing her way, running out of fuel, and crashing into the sea.

Internet Sources

John P. Riley Jr., "The Earhart Tragedy: Old Mystery, New Hypothesis," *Naval History,* August 2000, www.usni.org/NavalHistory/Articles00/nhriley.htm.

This article focuses on the *Itasca*'s failings during the search for Earhart's lost plane.

Joanne Cavanaugh Simpson, "Looking for Amelia." *Johns Hopkins*, June 2002, www.jhu.edu/~jhumag/0602web/amelia.html. This article talks about Nauticos' efforts to find underwater wreckage of Earhart's plane near Howland Island.

Index

Picture Credits

Cover, © Bettmann/CORBIS

Associated Press/World Wide Photo, 59, 69

© Bettmann/CORBIS, 9, 19, 20, 30, 38, 41, 46, 49, 52, 55, 64, 71, 74

© CORBIS, 39, 43, 66, 75, 96

© Hulton Archive by Getty Images, Inc., 65, 78, 80

The Kobal Collection/The Picture-Desk, 70

Library of Congress, 24, 31

Courtesy of Radcliffe College, 12, 14, 15, 16, 17, 27

© Reuters/CORBIS, 83

Smithsonian, 32, 35, 50

TIGHAR/The Earhart Project, 90, 91

© Underwood and Underwood/CORBIS, 23

Steve Zmina, 56, 61, 85, 89

About the Author

A freelance writer for more than twenty years, Patricia D. Netzley is the author of nearly forty books for children, young adults, and adults. She also teaches fiction and nonfiction writing for the Institute of Children's Literature (www.InstituteChildrensLit.com), and she once worked as an editor for the University of California at Los Angeles (UCLA) Medical Center. Netzley lives in Southern California with her husband, Raymond; her teenage children, Matthew, Sarah, and Jacob; and a Boston terrier named Maya.